Nb   DCPL0000185676

941.66.

12|10

HISTORY & GUIDE

Armagh

D1476718

WITHDRAWN FROM STOCK
DUBLIN CITY PUBLIC LIBRARIES

HISTORY & GUIDE

Armagh

IAN MAXWELL

NONSUCH

I saw the mystic vision flow,
And live in men, and woods, and streams,
Until I could no longer know
The dream of life from my own dreams.

Extract from a poem by Æ Russell included on a montage of Lurgan's notable
landmarks which can be seen opposite the local railway station

First published 2009

Nonsuch Publishing
119 Lower Baggot Street
Dublin 2
www.nonsuchireland.com

© Ian Maxwell, 2009

The right of Ian Maxwell to be identified as the Author
of this work has been asserted in accordance with the
Copyrights, Designs and Patents Act 1988.

All rights reserved. No part of this book may be reprinted
or reproduced or utilised in any form or by any electronic,
mechanical or other means, now known or hereafter invented,
including photocopying and recording, or in any information
storage or retrieval system, without the permission in writing
from the Publishers.

British Library Cataloguing in Publication Data.
A catalogue record for this book is available from the British Library.

ISBN 978 1 8458 8951 7

Typesetting and origination by The History Press
Printed in Great Britain

Contents

Acknowledgements

Grateful thanks to Dr Ken Abraham, Newry and Mourne Museum; Dr Greer Ramsey, Armagh County Museum; the staff of Craigavon Museum, Navon Fort and the Public Record Office of Northern Ireland for all their help in supplying photographs and other material. Thanks also to Jim Lyttle for his advice and support.

A very special word of thanks to my wife Valerie for her patience and eye for detail while taking all of the comtemporary photographs in this book. To my sons Scott and Callum; thanks for not making too much fuss about some very unusual excursions – it really isn't my fault that County Armagh doesn't have a beach!

And finally, my grateful thanks to Maeve, Stephanie and all the staff at Nonsuch Publishing for their encouragment.

Top left: Armagh View.

Top right: Old postcard.

Above left: Old postcard.

Above right: Jam Whittin's cottage.

Left: St Patrick's Church of Ireland Cathedral.

Chapter One

Historical Introduction

Despite being the smallest county in Northern Ireland, Co. Armagh is a region of amazing contrasts. It is the Orchard County, a famous fruit-growing area and its rich rolling hills have something of the appearance of the English shires. It was also the industrial heartland of mid–Ulster; its linen was exported all over the world and its rapidly expanding towns and villages clustered around its mills and factories. To the north is the marshy land that forms part of the Lough Neagh basin. To the south the county is more hilly, rising to the imposing mountains of the border region, the home of legendary heroes such as Finn McCool. And of course, it is celebrated as the Primatial County, with the Primates of the Church of Ireland and the Roman Catholic Church living beside their respective Cathedrals within the ancient city of Armagh.

'Armagh is perhaps the most important county in Ulster from the tourist's point of view', declared the Ulster Tourist Development Association in 1935:

> He who would know the story of Ulster or even of Ireland must begin his studies in the ecclesiastical capital, for from the City of Armagh, Ireland's Canterbury, in every age messengers have gone forth carrying and bringing back tidings which have opened and closed chapter after chapter in the history of Ireland.

It is certainly the case that much of Ulster's colourful early history has taken place in and around the ancient ecclesiastical settlement of Armagh. The name is the English version of the Irish *Ard Macha* , 'the Hill of Macha', the legendary queen who built her fortress about 600 BC on the hill around which the city would develop. More than 600 years later, another queen of that name built the palace of *Emain Macha* a few miles from the city at the site now known as Navan Fort. It became the ancient seat of the Kings of Ulster, and location for the legendary exploits of Cúchulainn and the Red Branch Knights. After the destruction of Navan, the centre of power moved to the present site of Armagh, probably in the fourth century AD.

Leabharlanna Poibli Chathair Bhaile Átha Cliath
Dublin City Public Libraries

In around AD 445, St Patrick persuaded Daire, the local Chieftain, to grant him the hilltop site where Macha had established her fortress nearly 1,000 years before. Patrick established his most important church at this site and around it colleges and schools were founded so that it became a centre of learning from which missionaries were sent to England and the Continent. It was the association with St Patrick which was the basis for Armagh's claim to be the ecclesiastical metropolis of Ireland. Dublin contested that claim over the centuries, and the matter had several times been sent to Rome for resolution by the Pope. Lord Deputy Strafford finally settled the issue to Armagh's satisfaction in 1634.

Until the end of the sixteenth century, Ulster remained unaffected by the piecemeal conquest of the rest of Ireland. Armagh was, however, on the edge of the most successfully anglicised colony in the island from the twelfth century. In 1177, John de Courcy and a small force of Norman knights had seized much of eastern Co. Down. To the north and west Gaelic culture and society remained intact. The O'Neills were the dominant family in Co. Armagh having by the thirteenth century driven out, among others, the MacMurphys from the barony of Fews, where they established their supremacy over the territory chiefly inhabited by the Garveys, O'Callaghans, and the Hanrattys. Meanwhile the Magennis, O'Hanlon, MacMahon, and O'Reilly lordships separated the O'Neills from the Anglo-Norman midlands and Co. Down coast.

During the fifteenth century Henry VIII extended his policy of surrender and re-grant into Ulster, where the frontier of mountain and lake had allowed the Gaelic system to remain intact. Gaelic chiefs were actively encouraged to surrender their lands to the king and have them re-granted (returned) if they swore loyalty to him. Those who surrendered were expected to speak English, wear English-style dress, remain loyal to the Crown, pay a rent, and follow English laws and customs. In 1542, Conn O'Neill accepted a royal grant of his lands with the title of the Earl of Tyrone. When Conn died in 1559 he was succeeded by his younger son, Shane, who assumed the traditional title of 'The O'Neill', and asserted his independence from the English Crown. He also managed to alienate his neighbours, the O'Donnells of Tyrconnell and the MacDonnells of north Antrim, and was defeated and killed in 1567.

For the next twenty years Armagh was relatively peaceful as Hugh O'Neill, Conn's grandson, established himself in the earldom. He had been brought up in England and, when war broke out between the crown and Shane O'Neill in 1566, had fought with the English forces. In 1585, he was formerly recognised by the Crown as the Earl of Tyrone, and in 1586, Armagh was made a county. With English influence in the region growing stronger, Tyrone declared himself, 'The

O'Neill' and was proclaimed a traitor. During the closing years of the reign of Queen Elizabeth I, a protracted and bloody war took place with the native Irish forces scoring a succession of victories over the English armies. A great battle was fought in 1598, between O'Neill's forces, assisted by those of O'Donnell and other chiefs, and the English forces commanded by Sir Henry Bagnall. The battle of the Yellow Ford took place two miles to the south of the city of Armagh where Bagnall and 800 of his men were killed, forcing English garrisons to withdraw from Armagh and Blackwater.

With the arrival of Lord Mountjoy as governor in 1600, the war began to turn in favour of the English Crown. By using a scorched earth policy which included devastating the Fews in south Armagh, Mountjoy undermined the Irish forces. Hugh O'Neill, Earl of Tyrone, surrendered shortly after the accession of James I in 1603. O'Neill signed the Treaty of Mellifont in 1603 and was allowed to retain his lands in Ulster. However, his position was undermined by the presence of English officials and garrisons stationed at Armagh and throughout his territories. Therefore in 1607, along with his family, retainers and fellow lords, he fled to the continent. Having reneged on their allegiance to the King, their lands were seized by the Crown, and in January 1608 a plan, which called for the plantation of much of Ulster, was published. In the plantation scheme for Co. Armagh, O'Neill was assigned to English undertakers, Lower Fews to Scottish undertakers and Orior to servitors (former soldiers) and natives. Trinity College was granted half of Armagh barony, and the other half went to the Church of Ireland and other servitors. The barony of Tiranny was given over to the church and to natives. Some natives were exempt from the plantation. One of the most prominent was Sir Turlough MacHenry O'Neill who was granted the barony of Upper Fews.

In an area devoid of large-scale urban settlement, Armagh became the county capital, and Charlemont and Mountnorris, both the location of English garrisons, were initially earmarked as major towns. Most of the major towns in Co. Armagh however were established during the plantation. These were usually established by the new landowners on their estates. Lurgan, Portadown, Loughgall, Richhill, Markethill, and Newtownhamilton were all established in this way. Later, in the nineteenth century, many towns and villages would develop around a mill or factory. Milford, a few miles west of Armagh city, grew up around the McCrum weaving factory, while the village of Laurelvale was founded in the 1850s by Thomas Sinton, to house the workers in his linen mill. Best known is the model village of Bessbrook, which was founded by John Grubb Richardson in 1845 with spacious squares surrounding the large linen mill owned by the Quaker family.

As a result of the plantation, the native Irish were to be heavily concentrated

Irish Rising, 1641.

in the south Armagh area and they retained the Irish language and their Catholic religion. The north of the county was dominated by a Protestant, English-speaking community. It is therefore hardly surprising that so much of the violence that accompanied the 1641 Rising took place in that area. In 1641, a number of Irish chieftains, who had earlier been dispossessed of their land or feared that such a fate was about to befall them, attempted to drive the settlers from Armagh as Ulster was plunged into more than ten years of bloody fighting. In the course of the campaign the town of Lurgan and the castles at Markethill and Tandragee were destroyed.

In the summer of 1649, Oliver Cromwell arrived in Ireland with an army with the object of regaining control of Ireland and avenging the colonists who were massacred in 1641. This he did with characteristic ruthlessness. During the Cromwellian confiscations that followed, 34 per cent of the land in Co. Armagh was seized and granted to soldiers and 'adventurers' who had subscribed towards the cost of the reconquest of Ireland. Most soldiers sold their land cheaply to their officers and returned to their homes. At the same time many Catholic tenants drifted back to the confiscated territories. Nevertheless, Catholic landowners had been replaced by army officers and those Protestant landowners already established since the plantation. They were reinforced by a new wave of immigrants towards the end of the century. The new settlers were divided into those, usually of English desent, who were Church of Ireland, and those lowland Scots, who brought with them their Presbyterianism. Generally speaking the northern portion of the county was dominated by the established Church while the Presbyterians dominated the middle third.

The distribution of names in Co. Armagh illustrates the limited success of the plantation in subsequent colonial settlement in the region. The most popular surnames are almost equally divided between native Irish and settler surnames. Murphy, the most common surname throughout Ireland, is also the most popular found in Co. Armagh. This is followed by Hughes; Wilson and Campbell, representing settler families; then by the native Irish name, O'Hare, and Smith, the commonest name in England and Wales. The Irish names McCann and Donnelly are followed alternatively by settler and Irish names. These are Watson, Quinn, Johnston, Kelly and Thompson.

Despite the prolonged wars of the seventeenth century that devastated much of its countryside, Co. Armagh was to become one of the most prosperous and densely populated counties in Ulster during the following century. Landlords such as Arthur Brownlow, the major landowner in the Lurgan area, encouraged their tenants to weave their linen yarn into cloth. He established a market at Lurgan and promised to purchase all the linen sold. Linens for local use had been woven in Ulster for centuries, but the industry assumed an international importance at the end of the seventeenth century. An English observer reported from Ulster in 1683:

> The Scotch and Irish in that province addicting themselves to the spinning of linen yarn, attained to vast qualities of that community, which they transported to their great profit, the conveniency of which drew thither multitudes of linen weavers, that my opinion is, there is not a greater quantity of linen in like circuit in Europe.

North Armagh became the heart of the 'linen triangle', which extended to Dungannon to the west and Lisburn to the east. Between 1776 and 1778 the prominent agriculturist Arthur Young toured Ireland. He found that the farms in Co. Armagh were very small and given over to linen manufacture. At Maghan he had a chance to take a close look at the everyday life of the weaver:

> Their food is stir-about, potatoes, bread of maslin [i.e. mixed grain] or wheat, and some meat once a fortnight. They are well clothed and have plenty of fuel. The weavers universally earn much more than the few labourers there are...As to health, from the sedentary life, they rarely change their profession for that. They take exercise of a different sort, keeping packs of hounds, every man one, and joining; they hunt hares: a pack of hounds is never heard, but all the weavers leave their looms, and away they go after them by hundreds.

The linen industry also encouraged continuous migrations of settlers into Co. Armagh during the eighteenth century. Arthur Young found that:

> Scarce any of them have potatoes and oats to feed their families; great importations from Louth, Meath, Monaghan, Cavan and Tyrone, besides what comes occasionally from England and Scotland.

This very prosperity contributed to the intense rivalry in the county between the Catholic and Protestant populations which were almost equal in numbers. Faction fighting between rival groups developed into sectarian conflict. In north Armagh strong Catholic parishes clashed with neighbouring Protestant parishes. This had taken on a more organised form by the late seventeenth century in the Protestant Peep-o'-Day boys and Catholic Defenders which culminated in the 'Battle of the Diamond' in September 1795. This famous Protestant victory led to the formation of the first Orange lodges and the movement has continued to enjoy much support in north Armagh to this day. Chevalier De Latocnaye, a former Royalist Officer of Cavalry, who was forced to flee his native France because of the Revolution, visited Ireland in the mid-1790s. He found the Armagh countryside much disturbed and blamed the trouble on the high quality of the agricultural land and the quarrelsome nature of the locals:

> This country, which is, certainly, the most beautiful in Ireland, is also that in which the inhabitants are the least tractable, and approach nearest to the character which the English call "Wild Irish". The animosity between the different sects certainly contributes to this savagery, but if this pretext for it were not available, another would soon be found. The real reason is that the fertility of the country attracted a great many strangers, who, having multiplied exceedingly, have become too numerous to allow of equitable division of the land with the descendants of the ancient stock, and therefore wish to expatriate these, and to remain alone the occupiers. The others, naturally, wish to see the expulsion of the colonists or settlers, and the land remaining in their sole possession. Hence the continual quarrels between neighbours, such as are not found elsewhere. Sides are taken, disputes multiply, the sticks rattle, and the side which the Government for the moment favours profits by the sense of protection, and does its best to inflict the greatest possible injury on the other.

Despite the intense sectarian rivalry, the population of the county continued to grow after the Napoleonic Wars during the late eighteenth and early nineteenth centuries which led to an increase in the price of agricultural produce. Sir Charles Coote in his survey of 1804, wrote that, 'Armagh is indisputably, in proportion to its size, the most populous county in Ireland. Although much of the surface is covered with mountains, yet the greater part of the wildest country is very thickly inhabited, and it is on this account that its superior population is allowed.' He was most impressed by the quality of life enjoyed by the people of the county commenting, 'I must confess, that the extraordinary comforts, so eminently enjoyed by the people of this county, both of the middle and the lower class, was a matter of astonishment to me, who had been well acquainted with the relative situation of those classes in other counties in this province, where their pursuits, both in and out of doors, so exactly corresponded.' He put this down to the fact that 'more money can be earned by the manufacture of fine, than of coarse linen; Armagh being more engaged in fine webs, than the other counties of Ulster which lie west of it.' More improbably he found that the people were, 'more industrious and sober, and their earnings are seldom spent in the dram-shop.'

William Makepeace Thackeray, author of *Vanity Fair*, also noticed a change in the character of the people from those he had encountered further south. However, his impressions of the people of Co. Armagh were largely gathered on his coach trip one Sunday evening as he made his way from Armagh to Belfast, and from an encounter with a northern and southern waiter he had come across at an inn at Armagh:

> the girls have their hair neatly braided up, not loose over their faces as in the south; and not only are bare feet very rare, and stockings extremely neat and white, but I am sure I saw at least a dozen good silk gowns upon the women along the road, and scarcely one which was not clean and in good order. The men for the most part figured in jackets, caps, and trousers, eschewing the old well of a hat which covers the popular head at the other end of the island, the breeches and the long ill-made tail coat.

He also found the accent very different. 'The people speak with a Scotch twang, and, as I fancied, much more simply and to the point'.

A feature of the Co. Armagh countryside that has remained to this day is the patchwork of small farms which dominate the landscape. The success of the linen industry in the county had enabled many weavers to take on small farms to supplement their income. Coote commented on this, 'The soil being excellent, the pursuit of manufacture, and the population very numerous, are the causes of the small size of farms, which are of so little extent as to leave the average of the county at less than five acres'. It is worth taking a drive to the top of Carrigatuke Mountain on the road from Markethill to Keady, where this landscape of small farms and abundant hedgerows can still be seen.

Mr and Mrs Hall, who toured Ireland in 1840, were impressed by what they saw of the county:

> while it may be surpassed by many in picturesque beauty, it is surpassed by none in the sturdy, independent character of its peasantry. Along the high roads and also among the by-ways very little poverty is encountered; the cottages are for the most part neat, clean and comfortable, and few of then are without orchards added to the ordinary garden, and the continual click-clack of the shuttle betokens the industry that is securing humble luxuries within, and the whole of its inmates, from the very aged to the very young, are made useful in some degree.

Within a few years of Mr and Mrs Hall's visit the county was devastated by the impact of the Great Famine. Much of County Armagh was severely affected by the desolation caused by the potato blight and the fever that followed in its wake.

In 1845, the potato crop had been badly affected by the blight, however, when in July and August 1846 it struck again, the impact throughout the county was ruinous. The workhouses, set up to deal with the destitute poor that were a feature of Ireland at the time, were soon overwhelmed. Henry John Porter, agent on the Duke of Manchester estates at Tandragee and Portadown, described the devastation cause by the blight in a letter to Sir T. Freemantle, Dublin Castle, dated 27 October 1845:

> Having returned from Dublin on Saturday night I was anxious to ascertain the state of potato crops on the farm of [the] Duke of Manchester's within his demesne and find the greater part of the crops had been dug, and put into pits or bins in the field and a portion housed. The steward had got some put up in this way about 10 days ago and on opening the pits they were found to be in a state of decomposition, and a smell that of decayed refuse from the garden.

As the year 1846 progressed, the prospect looked good until mid-summer. However, the *Armagh Guardian* of 4 August of that year, carried the ominous report:

> Captain Rodgers of Eden House, Loughgall, informs us that he examined a large field of his potatoes on Wednesday last, at which time they had a most healthy and luxuriant appearance. On the Friday following he again examined them, and the tops were completely blighted. Several other persons in the same neighbourhood have furnished us with similar intelligence.

The distress brought about by the famine was all the more marked, for it happened during a slump in the linen and cotton trade putting further pressure on families already suffering from the impact of rapid industrialisation. According to a reports received by the Central Relief Committee of the Society of Friends (the Quakers), many parts of County Armagh were in deep distress. One report of February 1847 records the following:

> I have myself witnessed the living lying on straw, by the side of the unburied dead, who had died three days before. Many cases of deaths from actual starvation have occurred amongst the able-bodied, without reckoning the aged and infirm, who have been cut off by the effects of starvation, or the very many children who have died from the same cause. I have been called to see a girl of four years old, a few weeks ago a strong healthy girl, who was so emaciated as to be unable either to stand or move a limb. I have visited

houses where there was no article whatever of food or clothing, nothing but straw to lie down upon, not even a stool to sit upon, some of whose inmates, I fear, must have perished. Last year, to have been buried without a hearse, would have been a lasting stigma to a family; now, hearses are almost laid aside. We are, in short, rapidly approaching, and if unassisted, must arrive at a state parallel to the worst pictures that have been presented to the public from the county of Cork.

The area served by Lurgan Poor Law Union suffered greatly throughout the Famine of 1846-48. Fever, as usual, followed in the wake of the famine and relief committees were empowered to provide temporary hospitals, to ventilate and cleanse cabins, and to procure the proper burial of the dead. By 1847 almost every person admitted into workhouses were patients suffering from either dysentery, fever, or were in the early stages of disease. There were also casualties among the boards of guardians including the Chairman of Lurgan Board of Guardians, Lord Lurgan, who died from the fever in 1847. The death rate in Lurgan workhouse was so appalling that at the end of January 1847, the Poor Law Commissioners demanded an explanation. Dr Bell, the medical officer, wrote in reply:

Many diseases are now prevalent in the country, and the great majority of new admissions are, when brought into the house, at the point of death, in a moribund state. Many have been known to die on the road, and others on being raised from their beds to come to the workhouse have died before they could be put into the cart, and numbers have died in less than 24 hours subsequent to their admission … many dying persons are sent for admission merely that coffins may be obtained for them at the expense of the Union.

The number of deaths in Lurgan workhouse had risen sharply during the month of January 1847, rising from eighteen for the week ending 2 January, to sixty-eight by the end of the month. In a letter of 19 February 1847 to Lord Lurgan, Chairman of the Board of Guardians, the Protestant chaplain, the Revd W.P. Oulton, blamed the 'dreadful mortality which has swept our workhouse' largely on the poor quality of food given the inmates; the bread was, 'very dark-coloured, not sufficiently baked, probably that it might weigh the heavier, and it was sour'. The broth was made of unsound beef which, according to ward-master Lutton, 'was so offensive, when cutting it up after being boiled he could hardly stand over it'.

The impact of the Great Famine can be seen in the dramatic fall in the population. There was considerable emigration from the county, which suffered great devastation as a result of the subsequent fever. In 1821, the year of the first properly-organised census, the population of County Armagh stood at 197,427. Within twenty years it had reached 232,393. By 1851, the first census to be held after the most catastrophic years of famine and fever, the population had fallen by more than 15 per cent to 196,084. It continued to fall until the Second World War. Although the 1951 census returns showed an increase in the pre-war figures by 5 per cent, the population figure stood at 114,254, less than half that of 1841.

During the late 1840s, and in the years immediately after the Great Famine, some families were evicted from their smallholdings by landlords in need of rents which could not be paid, or anxious to consolidate the farms on their estates. Many sought employment in Lurgan and Portadown, which had become manufacturing centres. Lurgan's population, numbering 2,207 in 1820 had more than doubled by the end of the Great Famine, and by 1888 was somewhere in the region of 15,000. Portadown also grew rapidly during the nineteenth century. In 1816 its population was estimated to be 600, while the *Belfast and Ulster Street Directory* for 1897 calculated that it reached 10,000. The ancient city of Armagh, better known for its architecture than its industries, also continued to grow, but at a much less dramatic rate that its northern rivals.

By the end of the nineteenth century, Co. Armagh was to become one of the major centres for opposition to the Home Rule Bills, which sought to give a measure of self-government to Ireland by establishing a parliament based in Dublin. During the late eighteenth century right through to the late twentieth century, north Armagh was a hotbed of sectarian conflict. The journalist, F. Frankfort Moore, published a book in 1914 in which he tried to explain the resistance to Home Rule in Ulster. He studied all aspects of the situation in the North and took a particular interest in the phenomenon of the sectarian riot. He noted that street fighting in Ulster was not carried out in a haphazard way. Moore described how he learned 'the proper way to conduct a street riot' in Portadown in 1869: 'Every boy and girl in the crowd understood the art thoroughly. When the police charged in military fashion, they hurried to one side or the other, refraining from obstructing them in the least, but returned immediately afterwards to the place they had occupied before the "charge"'.

With the partition of Ireland in 1921, Armagh was one of the six northern counties selected for a separate parliament in Belfast, which retained its close links with the rest of the United Kingdom. The sectarian conflict, which was a feature of Northern Ireland for much of the twentieth century, left its mark on many of the Province's towns and villages. South Armagh, one of the most beautiful stretches of countryside in Ireland, became better known as one of the world's trouble spots. The linen industry too went into decline, and the predominant role it played in the history and development of County Armagh is now largely remembered only in monuments such as abandoned mills and the magnificent mansions of the linen merchants.

The character of the county has changed with the decline of the linen industry, with the flax plant no longer dominating the countryside. H.V. Morton left a memorable description of the countryside as he travelled from Newry to Armagh, in the late 1920s:

> I went on all that afternoon through gentle country where the broad fields rose and fell on either side of me. Fields were full of millions of the minute flowers of the flax plant. In mid-August these crops are taken up and placed in bog-holes and ponds to rot. They are then spread lightly over the fields to dry. This simple process removes the woody portions of the plant and makes it a stem of dry, hair-thin fibres. Before it can be called 'fax', as it is known to the spinning mills, it goes through a further refining process in a 'scutch mill'. But no lovelier sight is to be seen in an Ulster field than flax in bloom. They call it 'lint' and have a charming phrase to describe it in mid-summer – 'when lint is in the bell.'

Armagh remains, nevertheless, a place of myth and legend, and, away from the busy roads which transact the county, retains its charm particularly at apple blossom time. The city of Armagh remains the ecclesiastical capital of Ireland, and many of its finer buildings have been preserved and its history highlighted in a number of museums and visitors centres. In its publication, *Ulster 1935*, the Ulster Tourist Development Association boasted of Armagh City:

> In the straggling, hilly streets of this beautiful old city you may spend many happy hours. But you must not go alone. It is a place for those who need the company of another, for whom the charm of old things is increased a hundred fold, if some kindred spirit feels it too.

The same holds true in the twenty-first century.

Chapter 2

From Lough Neagh to Lurgan

It seems oddly fitting that Co. Armagh to the north should merge with the waters of **Lough Neagh**, because the Lough, like the county itself, is a place of myth and legend. From the Irish *Loch nEathach* meaning 'Eochu's lake', Lough Neagh is the largest freshwater lake in Britain and Ireland. Legend has it that the giant Finn MacCool created the Lough by tearing out a piece of turf and hurling it into the Irish Sea, creating the Isle of Man in the process. According to another legend, Lough Neagh is named after Eochu, son of Mairidh, a Munster prince who was drowned when a well overflowed to form the lake in the first century AD. In fact, the Eochu who gave name to Lough Neagh, appears to have been the mythical progenitor of the sept of Ui Eachach, 'descendants of Eochu', who inhabited the region in ancient times. In the late sixteenth and early seventeenth centuries, unsuccessful attempts were made to re-name the lake Lough Sidney and Lough Chichester after Lord Deputies Sir Henry Sidney and Sir Arthur Chichester respectively.

Local tradition maintains that down deep, under the waters of Lough Neagh, those with fairy vision can still see the columns and walls of the beautiful palaces once inhabited by the fairy race when they were the gods of the earth; and this tradition of a buried town beneath the waves has been prevalent for centuries among local people. In his tour of Ireland in the late twelfth century, Giraldus Cambrensis wrote that in his time the tops of towers, 'built after the fashion of the country,' were distinctly visible in calm, clear weather, under the surface of the lake.

The Lough as depicted in the ancient Irish annals was a place of fear and violence. According to the annals, the Vikings pillaged Louth from Lough Neagh in AD 840. In AD 928 a fleet of Vikings, led by the son of Ailche, also plundered the islands of Lough Neagh and its borders. The *Annals of Ulster* tell us that in the year 945, the 'foreigners' of Lough Neagh were killed and their fleet destroyed by Donnall and his brother, sons of Murtagh.

Today the **Lough Neagh Discovery Centre**, situated within the Oxford Island National Nature Reserve just off the M1 motorway, is an excellent starting point for any visit to Lough Neagh. With its superb setting on the shores of Lough Neagh, the centre is a required visit for anyone wishing to enjoy the natural beauty of the lough shore and its abundant wildlife. Oxford Island, thought by many to be of Norse origin, is in fact a corruption of Hawksworth's Island, named after a Captain Robert Hawksworth, who is recorded as a tenant of the Brownlow estate here in 1666.

A few miles to the west on the lough shore is the village of **Maghery**, *An Machaire* 'the plain', located between the estuaries of the Blackwater and Bann rivers, which are only two miles apart. Lying two miles from the M1 motorway, the village consisting of just over 200 residents, appears to the visitor to be a recent development. In fact, in the graveyard attached to Maghery Chapel there are the remains of one of the old granges of the Abbey of St Peter and St Paul at Armagh. Maghery, as visited by Richard Hayward just before the Second World War, was a popular spot for tourists:

> Inshore there is Maghery, a nice little lakeshore village with a fine hotel. For Maghery has become an important tourist centre, offering rowing and sailing on Lough Neagh, quite good bathing, duck and widgeon shooting, and fast-and-furious pike, perch and bream fishing in the Blackwater which here enters the great lake.

Today this part of Co. Armagh seems sadly neglected by tourists. It is ironic, given the fact that it was emigrants from Maghery village who gave New York's Coney Island its name: and at the Birches nearby, Thomas Jackson, grandfather of the famous American General Stonewall Jackson, was born and lived until he emigrated to the United States.

Maghery Country Park, situated on the shores of Lough Neagh, covers an area of 30 acres comprising woodland walks and picnic areas in natural surroundings. It is also from here that a boat leaves each Sunday for the more important of the Lough Neagh islands, **Coney Island**. Sailing across the Lough to Coney Island, the distant shape of Slemish Mountain rises out of the mist. It takes only five minutes to reach the heavily wooded island. The visitor is greeted by the remains of a tower used by Shane O'Neill as a lookout post and stronghold in the early sixteenth century. Surrounded by bluebells, it is now a remarkably tranquil spot and an appropriate place for the remains of James Alfred Caulfield, the seventh Viscount and eleventh Baron of Charlemont, who built a Victorian summer cottage on the island in 1895. The cottage has been renovated in recent years and is now the private home of the island's warden.

O' Neill's Tower, Coney Island.

O' Neill's Tower, Coney Island.

Above left: Coney Island cottage.

Above right: St Patrick's Stone, Coney Island.

Archaeologists have carried out many excavations on the island and have found evidence of continual human occupation since Mesolithic times, approximately 8,500 years ago. The island is presently 8 acres in size, but it is still easy to see the old shoreline which existed before the Lough was lowered. Close to the warden's cottage is St Patrick's Stone. This was traditionally believed to be the spot where St Patrick rested when he visited the island in the fifth century. He supposedly walked to the island by using a ford called St Patrick's Road which stretched from the mainland. The ford was removed during the nineteenth century to help barge navigation on the Lough. The island also contains the remains of a Norman motte. This was built as a defensive stronghold during the thirteenth century and is one of the most westerly Anglo-Norman outposts in Ulster.

A few miles to the south of Maghery, is the **Montaighs** (pronounced munches), an area known for its peat cutting. In Irish the name is derived from *Na Mointeacha* which means, appropriately enough, 'the bogs/moors'. Mr and Mrs Hall visited the area early in the 1840s:

In driving to the magnificent Lough Neagh from our headquarters in the neighbourhood of Portadown, we passed through a singular district called the 'Munches'. Let the reader imagine a tract of bog stretching far and away; carriage and cart road have been formed through it at great expense, and yet the only change of soil is from bad bog to good bog, from turf so black and hard that its very sight gladdens the housewife's heart, to poor pale brown crumbling stuff, which the poor burn because they can afford no better. Squatters are numerous, but they have managed to cultivate patches of this arid common into productive land.

With the destruction of so much of Armagh's native woodland in the fifteenth and sixteenth centuries, peat was a major source of fuel. The right to cut peat on small plots of land (known as turbary rights) were allocated to local landowners, and extensive records known as 'Bog Rentals' can be found in many estates, collections deposited in the Public Record Office of Northern.

To get a better idea of the importance of peat to the local economy a visit to the **Peatlands Country Park** is a must. Just off the MI motorway between Portadown and Dungannon, it is the first of its type in the British Isles and was specifically established to promote and facilitate peatland awareness and issues. The park is rich in insects, particularly butterflies, moths, dragonflies, and damselflies. Many woodland and wetland birds, and several species of waterfowl, nest here. Red and grey squirrels, badgers, and hares are also present, while lizards and newts can be found in the open bog areas. The Peatlands Park narrow-gauge Railway has been associated with the area since the 1950s and is a big attraction for the young and old alike. The new locomotive can take up to seventy passengers at a time on a 1.5km journey through leafy tunnels and restored open bog.

Above: Lord Charlemont's grave, Coney Island.

Right: Lord Charlemont's grave, Coney Island.

A few miles to the south of Lough Neagh is the town of **Lurgan** near the County Down border. With a population of approximately 38,000, it is the first major town encountered in north Armagh. Lurgan, from the Irish, *An Lorgain* meaning 'the long ridge', is characteristic of many Ulster Plantation settlements, with its straight, wide planned streets and rows of two-story Victorian houses. Once in O'Neill's land, Lurgan, or the parish of Shankill, was forfeited to the Crown after the flight of the Earls, and in 1609, John and William Brownlow were given 1,500 and 1,000 acres respectively to 'plant' with English families. By 1619, John was dead, and William was in possession of the lands. According to Pynnar's Survey of that year, a very fair town had been established consisting of forty-two houses, all inhabited by English families, with streets paved clean through. There were also two water-mills and a windmill, all for corn, and a store of arms in the manor. In 1641, the town was attacked and destroyed by raiding parties under the Macans, Magennises, and the O'Hanlons, who murdered several inhabitants. The town had barely recovered from this catastrophe, when the overthrow of James II in England brought renewed warfare to Ireland. Once again Lurgan was attacked and destroyed.

After the Battle of the Boyne, King William III granted a patent for fairs and markets in the town, which played a major role in its return to prosperity. By 1703, Lurgan was described as:

> a large village consisting of a great many stone houses well shingled and finished and abounding with a great number of British inhabitants who are industrious and trading people who have considerably advanced and improved the several manufactures and especially the linen manufacture there and is…one of the most thriving and flourishing villages and a most considerable market town in the province of Ulster.

The Brownlow family were known for their religious tolerance and allowed many Roman Catholic tenants to hold land and also permitted a significant colony of members of the Religious Society of Friends (Quakers) to thrive. These Quaker colonists, mainly disenchanted former Cromwellian soldiers from Yorkshire and Cumberland, were prominent in the early development of the linen industry, especially in bleaching.

Dr Thomas Molyneux visited the town in the early eighteenth century, and his recollections were published in *Journey to ye North*, in 1708. He considered Lurgan:

> at present the greatest mart of linen manufactories in the north, being almost entirely peopled with linen weavers, and all by the care and cost of Mr. Brownlow, who on his first establishing the trade here, bought up everything to the market of cloth (linen)

and lost at first considerably, but at length the thing fixing itself, he is now by the same methods a considerable grainer. This gentleman is more curious than ordinary and has by him several old Irish manuscripts which he can read and understand very well. He showed me one in parchment of the Bible (as I remember) pretended to be written by St. Patrick's own hand but this must be a fable.

In fact, the Brownlow family had in its possession, *The Book of Armagh*, written in a monastery at Armagh towards the beginning of the ninth century AD. It is a copy of the New Testament in Latin, and bound up with it is the *Confessio* of St Patrick. At the end of the *Confessio,* the scribe Ferdomnach wrote, 'Thus far the volume which Patrick wrote with his own hand', indicating that he had access to a copy of St Patrick's originally manuscript which is now lost. *The Book of Armagh* remained in the Brownlow family until 1853, when it was sold to the Irish antiquary, Dr William Reeves, who was at that time librarian of the Robinson Library, Armagh. Against all odds it has survived for more than 1,000 years, and today is held by Trinity College, Dublin.

For centuries after the Plantation, Lurgan preserved its very English character as noted by the author of *A Tour Through Ireland* published in 1780:

> This is one of the prettiest little market towns in the kingdom. The inhabitants are genteel, sensible and friendly. They seem, indeed, to exert themselves to support the reputation of their town which, from the similarity of its inhabitants to those of the English, had for many years acquired the name of Little England, and an Englishman at Lurgan indeed will think himself in his own country.

By the nineteenth century Lurgan had become a major industrial centre. Lurgan can justly claim to be one of the pioneers in the introduction of linen power-loom weaving. James Malcolm built his power loom factory in 1855, and in 1866 he also established the first factory in the United Kingdom for hemstitching of linen by machine. Johnston, Allen & Co. at the peak period of the handloom trade gave employment to upwards of 1,000 weavers. In 1888, they built a power-loom weaving factory and warehouse in Victoria Street and its red brick tower can still be seen from the train as it approaches Lurgan station. Sadly none of the great spinning mills in Lurgan are still in operation.

Lurgan's Victorian prosperity was underlined by the opening of Lurgan railway station on 18 November 1841. At the top of William Street, which connects Lurgan with its railway station, a blue plaque commemorates the birthplace of George Russell, writer, editor, critic, poet, and painter. Russell, the youngest of three children, was born in William Street, Lurgan, on 10 April 1867. His father, Thomas Elias Russell, came either from Co. Tyrone, or Drumgor in Armagh, and was a bookkeeper employed by Bell and Co., a Quaker firm of cambric manufacturers. His mother, Marrianne Russell (*née* Armstrong), was from Co. Armagh. For much of its history Lurgan has had an unenviable reputation for religious fanaticism. All his life Russell remembered how, 'at any time a chance word might provoke a battle, and a whole horde of wild fanatics lying in ambush might rush out of the doors at a signal given, and in the name of God try to obliterate His image on each other's faces'.

Johnston & Allen factory, Lurgan.

George Russell (Æ)

Soon after his birth, the family moved to a cottage just within the entrance of Lord Lurgan's grounds. The Russell children attended the Model School, where George, who was not quite four years old, did well in writing and drawing. According to one of his friends, a master told him fairy stories which made a lasting impression. In later life he remembered having a quite ordinary childhood, and took pleasure in spending his own money when he reached the age of five or six. He later recalled that he had a taste for penny dreadfuls about the Wild West, and a childhood, 'made lurid by pirates and highwaymen and detectives and Red Indians'.

In 1878, Russell's father accepted an offer of employment from his friend Robert Gardiner, who had a partnership in a firm of accountants, and the family moved to Dublin. Looking back Russell wrote, 'I was born in Lurgan ... and have never been sufficiently grateful to Providence for the mercy shown to me in removing me from Ulster, though I like the people I cannot breathe in the religious and political atmosphere of the North East corner of Ireland'. Nevertheless, from time to time he returned to Ulster on holiday. According to his friend Carrie Rea, who met him just after he left school, he spent a fortnight in Armagh City every two years, but in the alternative years he may have stayed on his maternal grandparent's farm at Drumgor, which he certainly visited.

Shankill Graveyard is located off William Street and just 300 yards from Lurgan town centre. It is now enclosed by three housing developments and the Belfast–Dublin railway line. This wonderful old graveyard was once a modest double-ring fort, the outline of which is still discernable. It is likely that the small church, which was erected on the mount in the centre of the fort, served as a parish church for the small community of the district. The old church was subsequently taken down, and the Brownlow family erected their burial vault on the site.

More than 11,000 people of Shankill Parish and beyond lie buried in the local graveyard, which was extended at the beginning of the nineteenth century. The most celebrated of these is unquestionably Marjorie McCall. Marjorie lived in Church Place in Lurgan during the early eighteenth century. Her husband John, a doctor, was distraught when she died following a short illness. He became even more distressed when he was unable to remove the ring she always wore. Grave robbing was not uncommon at the time and relatives feared that her final resting place would be desecrated, owing to the presence of the ring. Sure enough her body was exhumed shortly after the burial. Unconcerned about mutilating the corpse, thieves set about hacking off the ring finger. Much to the terror of the grave robbers, Marjorie woke from a deep coma and opened her eyes. Shortly afterwards, the grieving family members were surprised to hear a familiar knock on the door. Upon opening it, they found Marjorie restored to life and still dressed in her shroud. Marjorie finally died many years later and her body was returned to Shankill graveyard, where her headstone remains to this day inscribed with the words, 'Marjorie McCall: Lived Once, Buried Twice'.

The **church of Christ The Redeemer** is Lurgan's most recognizable landmark. Situated in Church Place, in the centre of Lurgan, its spire can be seen miles away from the town. Commenced in 1722, and opened for worship in 1724, this church was described in Lewis, 1837, as 'a handsome Grecian edifice with a lofty tower and octagonal spire'. A second phase of building in the 1860s has left us with the Victorian Gothic building we can see today. The original spire was destroyed in a fire in 1792. Henry Monro, who later lead the men of Down in the United Irish insurgents at the Battle of Ballynahinch in 1798, made heroic efforts to save the church. According to the *Belfast News Letter*:

> several times he exposed himself that the beholders turned their eyes away expecting to see him topple from his giddy heights amongst the burning ruins, and though the bell fell hissing from the belfry this brave man continued his efforts till the fire was reduced and the church safe.

After the fire the tower was raised by 20 feet and a new spire was added; these renovations were completed by 1801. By that time Henry Monro had been found guilty of treason and hanged in his home town of Lisburn.

Undoubtedly the most impressive building in Lurgan is **Brownlow House**. This was the county seat of the Brownlow family and was built in 1836 to a design by the Scottish architect, William Henry Playfair. The house was constructed in Scottish sandstone in the Elizabethan style and stood in an estate of some 259 acres, which includes a man-made lake of 53 acres. Brownlow House, which is reputed to have 365 rooms, was built for the Right Honourable Charles Brownlow, and until he was raised to the peerage in 1839, it was called Lurgan House. In 1893, the third Baron Brownlow sold the lake and house to Lurgan Borough Council in for the sum of £2000. In 1903, it was sold to the Lurgan District Orange Lodge and has now the distinction of being the largest Orange Hall in the world. During the First World War it was used as a training base for the 36th Ulster Division. At the commencement of the Second World War, the house was again utilised by allied forces, and in January 1942, it served as headquarters for the V (US) Army Corp followed, in September 1943, by the XV (US) Army Corp under the command of General George Patton. General Dwight D. Eisenhower is reputed to have stayed overnight in Brownlow House during this period.

There is a magnificent public park beside the town, in what was Lord Lurgan's demesne. **Lurgan Park** is the second largest public park in Ireland, the biggest being Phoenix Park in Dublin. An interesting feature of the park is the recently-restored Jubilee Fountain, dating from 1887, which was erected to celebrate fifty years of Queen Victoria's reign. The man-made lake, which is one of the great attractions of the park, was dug during the Famine as a means of creating jobs for the local people. At the time of its construction the lake was one of the largest hand-dug lakes in Ireland. During its construction the term 'Lurgan Spade' came into use. According to residents of the town, the workmen who were digging the lake worked for 1½ to 3d a day, less than ordinary rate of wages. The workers were known as the Spades, and due to the unpleasant nature of the work and their meagre rewards, they were repudiated to be particularly sombre. As a result anyone who looks particularly miserable is to this day described as, 'having a face like a Lurgan spade'.

Apart from the legacy of a magnificent park, the Brownlow family also left the town a sporting legend: Master McGrath, a greyhound, that won the Waterloo Cup three times in 1868, 1870, and 1871. This magnificent dog is still remembered in story and rhyme:

Above: Brownlow House, Lurgan.

Lurgan Lake.

As swift as the wind o'er the green fields she flew.

The hare she led on, what a beautiful view,

"Three cheers for old Ireland," said Master McGrath.

He jumped on her back and he held up his paw;

In the days that are gone and it can't be denied,

I've known many greyhounds that filled me with pride

But the greatest and the bravest the world ever saw

Was our champion of champions, brave Master McGrath

Behind the pulpit in the eighteenth-century parish church is a stained-glass window which bears his image. He is also remembered all over the town, including in its coat of arms. A statue of him was unveiled at Craigavon Civic Centre in 1993, over 120 years after his last glory in 1871. A festival is also held yearly in his honour.

Despite redevelopment and major terrorist attacks, the essential character of Lurgan's main street is much as it was 100 years ago. At the corner of High Street and Union Street stands the Mechanics Institute, a two-storey building which was opened in 1858. The clock tower is one of the main features of the town centre. Lurgan Town Hall in Union Street, built in 1868, has been refurbished in recent years. The majority of the town's notable buildings are its churches, reflecting the religious toleration of the Brownlow family. **High Street Methodist church** was opened in 1826, and extensively renovated in 1910. The present building has a simple classical façade. Methodism in Lurgan dates from the period of John Wesley's first visit in 1756. He left a fascinating account of a subsequent visit in 1762 when he met Mr Miller an inventor:

> Monday, April 26 – In the evening I preached to a large congregation in the market house at Lurgan. I now embraced the opportunity which I had long desired of talking with Mr. Miller, the contriver of that statue which was in Lurgan when I was there before. It was the figure of an old man standing in a case, with a curtain drawn before him, over against a clock which stood on the other side of the room. Every time the clock struck, he opened the door with one hand, drew back the curtain with the other, turned his head, as if look-ing round on the company, and then said with a clear, loud, articulate voice, "Past one, two, three," and so on. But so many came to see this (the like of which all allowed was not to be seen in Europe) that Mr. Miller was in danger of being ruined, not having time to attend his own business; so, as none offered to purchase it or reward him for his pains, he took the whole machine in pieces; nor has he any thought of ever making anything of the kind again.

Above: Lurgan High Street 1920s.

Left: Master McGrath.

Below: Mechanics Institute.

Above left: Lurgan Volunteer.

Above right: Parish church, Lurgan.

Wesley was obviously fascinated by Mr Miller's invention, and sought him out again when preaching at Lurgan in 1773:

> Monday, 14 June - After preaching at Lurgan, I inquired of Mr. Miller whether he had any thoughts of perfecting his speaking statue, which had so long lain by. He said he had altered his design; that he intended, if he had life and health, to make two which would not only speak, but sing hymns alternately with an articulate voice; that he had made a trial and it answered well. But he could not tell when he should finish it, as he had much business of other kinds and could give only his leisure hours to this. How amazing is it that no man of fortune enables him to give all his time to the work!

Unfortunately the secret of this great machine died with its inventor.

Presbyterianism arrived in Lurgan in the 1680s. High Street **First Presbyterian church** has a fine classical portico dating from 1860, although the first building here was erected in 1827. *Bassett's Guide* of 1888 described it as, 'A structure of considerable dignity, with a handsome portico. The interior is spacious, and tastefully appointed'. The interior has the traditional porch, containing twin curly staircases giving access to the galleries. These, spanning three sides of the hall, are carried on fluted columns with Ionic capitals. It remains one of Lurgan's most attractive buildings.

First Presbyterian church, Lurgan.

In 1829, Charles Brownlow, 1st Baron of Lurgan, gave a site in North Street for the erection of a Roman Catholic church. Completed in 1833, the original building was replaced by **St Peter's** which was constructed in a number of phases between 1867 and 1900 in the Gothic style and finally completed in 1927. The slender spire, built of Drogheda limestone and reaching almost 200 feet, is the tallest structure in the town. Inside it is a very traditional church. Sir Charles Brett described it in his *Buildings of County Armagh* as:

> a very seemly, sober and traditional church, with no jarring modernisms, or incongruous bondieuserie either. The old High Altar has been kept; the new free-standing one is wholly in keeping; pews, confessional boxes and stations of the cross are old-fashioned but pleasing. The high vaulted wooden ceiling, with clerestory below, is carried on grey polished marble columns interspersed with pointed arches. A refreshingly unspoiled church.

Lurgan was also a Quaker stronghold. The Religious Society of Friends, also known as 'Quakers' or 'Friends', originated in the north-west of England during the mid-seventeenth century. Regarded with suspicion by the government, the Quaker movement arrived in Lurgan during the 1650s. Lurgan records note the origins of twenty families who emigrated to Ulster during the seventeenth century; one is from Scotland, nine from Yorkshire, four from Cumberland, two from Lancashire, two from Northumberland, and one each from Westmoreland and Durham. A fine wrought iron gateway at the top of High Street leads into the **Friends Meeting House** and graveyard. With its Italianate façade, it dates largely from 1882. Hiding the meeting house from the main street is a terrace of late nineteenth-century, three-storey town houses built in local quarried blackstone. They have notable yellow brick dressing. The plague at No.88 denotes the birth place of James Logan, the Quaker Secretary to William Penn, founder of Pennsylvania, who became president of its council.

Quaker Meeting House, Lurgan.

Lynastown Graveyard.

A few miles from the town, is **Lynastown Graveyard**. When William Lynas, an early Quaker, died in April 1858, Quaker principles demanded a burial in unblessed or unconsecrated ground without the presence of an ordained priest. William's son, Thomas, buried his father in a plot of ground on his farm in Moyraverty. Others followed, and by the 1670s, it had become a Quaker cemetery. There are few gravestones; a minute of the London Yearly Meetings, in 1717, prohibited the use of gravestones and urged the removal of those already existing. It was not until 1850, that it was decided that plain headstones of uniform design were not inconsistent with Quaker principles. A large tablet has been provided, which contains the names of the 200 people interred in the cemetery. With the erection of a boundary wall and the planting of trees as is the Quaker custom, Lynastown graveyard is a magically tranquil spot on the fringes of Craigavon.

Chapter 3

South to Portadown

Five miles south from Lurgan is Portadown; north Armagh's other major industrial town. The road passes through **Craigavon**, an area consisting mainly of residential developments. Named after Sir James Craig, 1st Viscount Craigavon, who was Northern Ireland's first Prime Minister (1921-1940), it was designed as a new town in 1965, and intended to incorporate both Lurgan and Portadown, and two new sectors in between: Brownlow and Mandeville. The new sectors were named after the principal landowners in the area: the Brownlow family of Lurgan, and Mandeville, the junior title of the Dukes of Manchester, the largest landowners in the Portadown area.

The original plan was to encourage people to move out of Belfast and to ensure a more even distribution of industrial development across Northern Ireland. Some of the most striking innovations of the development included the separation of motor vehicles from pedestrians and cyclists, who were given their own dedicated path network, and the use of roundabouts instead of traffic lights at junctions. The new town was also provided with many amenities such as a leisure centre, shopping centre, civic centre, artificial lakes, playing fields, and an animal farm at Tannaghmore.

The hope for prosperity did not last long however. The area's main employer, Goodyear, Europe's largest factory, closed and the Troubles helped ensure that new investment failed to materialize. Consequently around 50 per cent of what was planned was never built, and of what was built, some of that had to be demolished after becoming empty and derelict. The inhabitants of Lurgan and Portadown also stubbornly held on to their separate identity, a rivalry that is particularly intense when the local football teams, Glenavon and Portadown, meet. In recent years, however, Craigavon has taken on a more prosperous appearance. The introduction of new estates have brought many new people into the area, and the expansion of the Craigavon Shopping Centre (now renamed the Rushmere Shopping Centre) has made it a major shopping destination.

Many visitors to the region today will be amazed to find out that what is now Craigavon has also many ancient associations. We know of two monasteries that were in existence before the Viking period. One of these was St Gobhan's, from which Seagoe takes its name; the other was St Evin's which gave its name to the townland of Taghnevan in Lurgan. The exact location of St Evin's monastery remains a mystery; we only know of its existence from the name, plus the fact that the ordnance surveyors noted about 1834, that there was a plot of ground in this townland that the pious locals never ploughed.

On the outskirts of Portadown, and fringed by Craigavon's housing developments, is **Seagoe parish church**. The ancient monastery established by St Gobhan was located at one of the oldest Christian settlements in Ireland dating from AD 540. The *Annals of the Four* Masters mentions in AD 700 that Gobhan had earlier built a house of prayer. The spot where Gobhan built his house was the little mound where the ruined church now stands in the cemetery in Lower Seagoe. It is still possible to discern where the old church ruin stands, and the outline of the large double-ringed rath, which formed the nucleus of the original foundations is still visible.

The first stone church is believed to have been built by settlers who came over from England with Lord Essex in the reign of Queen Elizabeth. It seems to have been attacked, for it is shown on a map of 1609 standing roofless among trees. Having been rebuilt, it was once again destroyed during the 1641 Rising. It was again rebuilt in the 1660s, however by the eighteenth century, the graveyard encroached more and more closely on the old walls. The belief that 'the nearer to the church, the closer to God' was common enough before the nineteenth century. This was further complicated by a long-standing custom in old Seagoe burials of carrying the coffin right around the church, so that it could be made to touch all four corners of the building. The effect of the encroaching graveyard severely curtailed the space about the church and, with each interment the ground steadily rose over the years so that on entering at the porch it became necessary to go down two steps to reach the level of the nave. As a result a new church, the current parish church, was constructed on an adjacent hill between 1814 and 1816.

Portadown, from the Irish *Port an Dunain*, 'landing place of the little fort', derived its name from the ancient castle of the McCanns or McCanes, who occupied this very important station commanding the pass of the River Bann. The landing place may have been for the ferry which crossed the Bann here before

Seagoe parish church.

the construction of the bridge in the early eighteenth century. At the time of the Plantation of Ulster, 1609, James I granted an extensive portion of land to William Powell. In 1625 this was confirmed to Prudence Obins and John Obins. They formed a settlement with fourteen English families and built a fine mansion in the Elizabethan style with turreted corners. The chief approach to the long disappeared Obins mansion was by way of the thoroughfare still known as Castle Street.

The main street of Portadown sweeps down to the bridge over the Bann and its importance to the development of the town was recently underlined when the bridge was widened. Although there were fords at Derrybrochus and Knock, the first mention of a bridge over the Bann was in the 1630s, when John Obins and Richard Cope built a primitive wooden structure. In October 1641, the bridge was the location for one of the most infamous events of the rising against the settler population. A group of Protestants were imprisoned in a church in Loughgall. They had been informed that they were going to be marched eastwards where they were to be expelled to England. The Irish soldiers were said by to be led by either Captain Manus O'Cane or Toole McCann – later accounts of the event differed on this point. After some time, the English civilians were taken out of the church and marched to a bridge over the River Bann. Once on the bridge, the group was stopped. At this point the civilians, threatened by pikes and swords, were forcibly stripped of their clothes. They were then herded off the bridge into the icy cold river waters at sword point. Most drowned or died of exposure, although some were said to have been shot by musket-fire as they struggled to stay afloat.

Estimates of the number of those killed varied from less than 100 to over 300. William Clark, a survivor of the massacre, said during the 1642 depositions that as many as 100 were killed at the bridge. As Clark was a witness of the massacre his figure is taken as being the most credible. The depositions record numerous reports of ghost sightings after the massacre. A woman named Elizabeth Price testified that she was present at Portadown Bridge and claimed to have seen at the spot of the massacre a spirit in the shape of a woman, 'her eyes seemed to twinkle in her head and her skin as white as snow ... divulged and then repeated the words "Revenge, Revenge, Revenge."'

The wide sloping main street of Portadown was noted for having a triangular 'square' at either end, but this has somewhat been obscured thanks to modern traffic management schemes. More than a dozen denominations have built churches and chapels in one small central area. There is a certain irony in this because when John Wesley, the founder of Methodism, visited the town in April 1767, he dismissed it, as 'a place not troubled with any kind of religion'. By 1888 *Bassett's Guide* could write:

Portadown is the great stronghold of Methodism in the County Armagh. The principal church is in Thomas Street. It is a specious edifice, and has a handsome portico, supported by four great pillars with Corinthian capitals. In the interior a gallery resting on thirteen ornamental pillars, runs all round. The front is tastefully ornamented, the pulpit is mahogany, and the Communion rails of the same wood. Over the pulpit there is a fine organ. The pews are modern and painted in oak ... The present Methodist Church was erected in 1860, and with the school-house attached, and minister's residence, coast about £5,000 ... The old church at the opposite side of the street, higher up, was built in 1832. It is now used for commercial purposes.

Old Seagoe church.

Left: Portadown
shopkeeper, 1892.

Below and opposite:
Portadown
Bridge.

St Mark's Church of Ireland is the focal point right in the centre of Portadown and local people often refer to it location simply as 'The church'. Many structural changes have been made since it was built in 1823. According to Basset, 'The style of architecture was early English, with square battlemented pinnacled tower. In 1885, the most important part of the edifice was remodelled, and the seating capacity enlarged by the addition of transepts. The church is now cruciform and the main roof groined.' Internally, Bassett commented, 'A beautiful pulpit ... constructed of Caen stone and marbles of Connemara, Cork, and Kilkenny, a lectern, with carved oak eagle, and a fine organ, are among the striking attractions.'

A mile to the north of Portadown is the much older parish church of **Dumcree**, a name familiar to many because of the sectarian clashes that occurred here during the 1990s. Drumcree (Irish *Droim Crí*) means 'ridge of the boundary', most likely referring to the River Bann. The site has been used for worship since the time of the Celts. The ancient parish of Drumcree was formed in 1110 comprising sixty-six townlands lying to the west of the Bann. It is unclear what happened to the church during the time of the Reformation, but a map of 1609, shows the church in ruins within the churchyard. Following the Ulster Plantation in 1610 a new church was built. This was described as, 'a plain stone building rough cast and whitewashed'. In 1812, a tower was built and in 1814, a church bell was installed. By 1854, it was decided to build a new church and this is the one that stands today.

Above: St Mark's, Portadown.

Left: Canal, Portadown.

By 1888, there were two congregations of Presbyterians in Portadown, one belonging to the first church, in Bridge Street, Edenderry, and the other to the Armagh Road church. The Edenderry church, built in 1857, has a handsome gable front, supported on two large corinthian columns. The Roman Catholic church is a large cruciform edifice, situated in William Street. According to Bassett, 1888:

> It has a high battlemented pinnacled tower, and altogether is quite imposing. The interior is rich in embellishments, and the effects harmonious and well calculated. Among the most noticeable features are the high altar, the Virgin's altar, and the pulpit, all in sculptured Caen stone, relieved by different coloured Irish marbles. As a work of art, the high altar is really meritorious.

From the time of the Obins Portadown developed slowly, until the introduction of the linen industry during the second half of the eighteenth century. The first noted industry was the manufacture of cider in 1682. In fact, it is recorded that Paul Le Harpur, cider maker to the Prince of Orange, was commissioned to provide cider for William's army on the way to the Boyne. It was not until 1762 when Michael Obins petitioned the Irish House of Commons to set up a linen market in Portadown, that the foundation for major industry was laid.

The arrival of the canal, started in Newry in 1730, and arriving in Portadown eleven years later, linking the town with both Carlingford Lough and Lough Neagh, also provided an important boost to local industry. The main reason for building the canal was the discovery of coal deposits at Coalisland, Co. Tyrone, and the need to transport them quickly to Dublin, at a time when road transport was difficult. The canal was 18 miles in length and travelled through the countryside between the towns of Newry and Portadown, passing Poyntzpass, Scarva, Madden Bridge, and Knock Bridge on the way. According to Sir Charles Coote in 1804:

> the entrance into this town from Lurgan gives a respectable idea of its wealth and the value of its local situation. The Bann navigation to Lough-Neagh crosses the road; the ware-houses on the banks of this river, and the numerous barges, display a considerable trade, with which the large brick houses and well assorted shops fully correspond.

The canal played a major role in Portadown's industrial development. According to the Ordnance Survey for 1838:

Corn-factors have established this place as a depot from its facility of communication with England by the Newry Canal. In consequence, it is the grain market for the surrounding country. Coals, both English and Irish, are kept by merchants for the supply of the town and surrounding neighbourhood. Turf is obtained in abundance from the bogs in this parish and is brought up the river from the Montiaghs.

Bassett's Guide, published in 1888, when the arrival of the railway had led to the decline of water transport, still underlined the canal's importance to the economy of the town:

> The carrying trade between Portadown, Newry and Belfast via, the Newry Canal, Lough Neagh and Lagan Canal, is still successful. The Newry Canal joins the Bann about an Irish mile south-east of the town, and continues the navigation system to Lough Neagh, 7 Irish miles. The Lagan Canal also joins Lough Neagh, so that vessels up to 70 tons burden may go from Belfast to Newry by way of Portadown. It takes one day to go to Newry from Portadown, light, and two days with cargo, going or returning. Freights, consisting of coal, grain, timber and general merchandize, are usually brisk enough to make the trade profitable for four individual boat owners, and four firms of boat owners…There are 13 locks. Nearly all the masters of boats share profits with the owners. About a third of the number live with their families on board the boats…At one time Portadown had direct communication by boat with Scotland and Wales. Belfast is now the limit.

The cargoes would have consisted of grain, imported timber, iron, English and Scotch coal, slates, Irish coal, flour, and oatmeal. By the 1880s, there were six quays and two slipways in the town, with a further five smaller ones between Robbs ferry, Derrybroughas, and Moyallon. Best known was Shillington's Quay, which was extensively used by Shillington's to bring in coal, building materials and hardware for their large wholesale and retail concern, which was in business in the town for more than a century and a half. Today, it is a favourite fishing spot, and its tranquil appearance is a world away from the busy scene it would have offered to Victorian visitors.

Newry Canal closed to navigation in 1947. Today the canal is used merely for drainage. There have been a number of unsuccessful attempts to attract funds to re-open the navigation. However, a pleasant walk along the towpath from Shillingston's Quay brings you to an atmospheric little spot known as **Moneypenny's Lock**, the last lock before the Newry Canal joins the Upper Bann River. It derives it name from Stephen Moneypenny who became lock-

Left: Shillington's Quay, looking toward Newry Canal *c.*1900.

Below: Newry Canal.

keeper around 1800, and whose family were lock-keepers for around eighty-five years. The restored eighteenth-century lock-keeper's house, stables and bothy offers visitors a glimpse of life on the canal in its heyday and information on the local wildlife.

Portadown's industrial development was hampered in the days before steam by the lack of a suitable water supply. According to the *Ordnance Survey Memoirs* in the 1830s:

> There are throughout the parish 4 corn mills turned by water and one by wind, 3 flax mills and a corn kiln. There is so little fall of water in the streams throughout this parish where mills do exist [that] the water is obtained by damming up and overflowing the adjoining meadows for 6 months in the year. From this want of water a flax mill is now building to be turned by steam.

It was the advent of steam power in the second half of the nineteenth century that led to the rapid industrial expansion of Portadown. According to Bassett:

> Within a comparatively short period, a change has been made in the methods of manu-facture at Portadown which threatens very soon to dispense entirely with the services of hand-loom weavers. Twenty years ago over 4,000 of these industrious hard-working people lived in the town and district. Good authorities agree that the number at present is now above 2,500. The young people are not following the occupation of their fathers to an appreciable extent, and a great many of the families have emigrated. The power-loom has been resisted as long as possible, but it has latterly been coming into fashion here with a rush. There are four large factories now in operation, giving employment between them to upward of 2,000 people, the majority of whom are females.

The success of the textile industry in Portadown led to a rapid increase in its pop-ulation; in 1819, the population stood at 900, by 1881 it had reached 7,850. The town, had by that time come into the possession of George Montagu, Viscount Mandeville, future 6th Duke of Manchester, when he married Miss Millicent Sparrow in 1822, and started an association with the Dukes of Manchester which, although severely diluted, still exists today in a small way. The Manchester's legacy to the town includes street names such as Montagu Street, Millicent Crescent, and Mandeville Street (the heir apparent to the Dukedom is styled Viscount Mandeville), in buildings such as the Fergus Hall (formerly the Duke's School and Church Street PS), and the Carlton Home (the Duke's former townhouse, latterly a maternity hospital/nurses accommodation and now private apartments).

Money Penny Arch Keeper's House.

At the top of the town, in front of St Mark's Church of Ireland, stands a granite pedestal and bronze standing figure, which was erected in 1910, to the memory of Colonel Edward James Saunderson. Saunderson was a Co. Cavan landowner who was elected MP for the North Armagh constituency after a fiercely contested election in 1885. Shortly afterwards he became leader of the newly-established Irish Unionist Party, a position he held until his death in 1906. Every 12 July, a traditional Orange Sash is draped around the shoulder of the Colonel in acknowledgement of his fight against Gladstone Home Rule Bills, which sought to establish a Parliament in Dublin, and his close association with the Orange Order.

Saunderson urged Ulster Unionists to take an independent line and warned them that they must be prepared to resist Home Rule and to use physical force if necessary. He was, however, conservative by nature and tended to avoid confrontation. His letters to his wife during the election of 1886, show that he was unprepared for the sort of full-blooded sectarianism which were the hallmark of a Co. Armagh election. Saunderson stood against the Nationalist candidate, James Williamson, and described the events which led up to a riot between the rival factions in Portadown. He spoke to his followers in front of St Mark's church, while his rival held a meeting a few hundred yards away. In a letter to his wife dated 8 July 1886, Saunderson writes:

> We were dragged by the people in a huge break to the Church where I spouted. Then off we went, still dragged, all round the town down near where my opponent was holding forth. A line of Police separated us from him so all the people would do was to vent their rage in yells of an awful description. Some, however, found out a way of turning the Police and gained a point of vantage where they could shell the rebel meeting with stones. This they did. The Police charged them but the people drove the Police back with great slaughter. Military were telegraphed for to Armagh but by the time they arrived it was all over.

In fact casualties were limited to sixteen policemen and two district inspectors wounded.

By the end of the nineteenth century Portadown was at the height of its prosperity. The extension of the Ulster Railway to the town in 1842 underlined Portadown's position as the transport capital of Co. Armagh. William Makepeace Thackeray arrived in the town shortly after the establishment of the railway. He recalled:

> The little brisk town of Portadown, with its comfortable unpretending houses, its squares and market-place, its pretty quay, with craft along the river, a steamer building on the dock, close to mills and warehouses that look in a full state of prosperity, was a pleasant conclusion to this ten miles' drive, that ended at the newly opened railway-station.

With the building of the railway bridge over the Bann in 1848, Portadown became a major railway junction for the main railway lines from Belfast, Dublin, Londonderry, Armagh, and the Irish midlands. The third and finest Ulster Railway station was built at Watson Street, Portadown in 1861-2, to a design by Sir John Macneill and incorporating four platforms as it did, was a fitting reflection of

St Marks and Saunderson
statue.

Portadown's status as a 'Grand Junction' of the railways from Belfast, Armagh, Newry and Dundalk, Omagh and Dungannon, as well as steamboat services across Lough Neagh, from Kinnegoe to Newport Trench and Ballyronan.

Sadly, Portadown's position as a major railway junction declined after the closure of the line to Armagh in 1957, and the services to Dungannon, Omagh, and Londonderry disappeared eight years later in 1965. The track which turned off sharply to the left was the main line to Dublin, and is the only one to survive to this day. It is also a source of regret to all local railway enthusiasts that the magnificent Victorian railway station in Portadown was demolished in the early 1960s to make way for an urban motorway. A new central station of little architectural merit was built in Woodhouse Street in 1970. There is little left at Watson Street to remind visitors that this was once a busy junction station that helped earn Portadown the title, 'The Hub of the North'.

A story, which first appeared in the *Journal of the Criagavon Historical Society* is still told of two commercial travellers who had to change trains late in the evening at Portadown. They enquired of a porter if they would have time to have a meal and on being told that they would, they adjourned to the refreshment room. The meal partaken, one looked at his watch and said, 'It's almost twenty to eight, we had better go for our train'. The other replied, 'I thought the porter said twenty past eight, let us check.' So they checked with the porter who replied, 'I didn't say twenty to eight and I didn't say twenty past eight. I said that you had twenty minutes to ate, and you have been ateing for half an hour, and you have missed your train.'

Chapter 4

West from Portadown

The busy A3 road takes the traveller from Portadown direct to Armagh. When Thackeray visited the area in 1842, he recalled that the ten miles from Armagh to Portadown was:

> not the prettiest, but one of the pleasantest, drives I have had in Ireland, for the county is well cultivated along the whole of the road, the trees in plenty, and villages and neat houses always in sight. The little farms, with their orchards and comfortable buildings, were as clean and trim as could be wished; they are mostly of one story, with long thatched roofs and shinning windows such as those that may be seen in Normandy and Picardy.

It is a scene which would have been familiar to travellers a century later. However, the closure of the railway line from Portadown to Armagh in 1957 has ensured that the A3 is a busy road, and the rural tranquillity experienced by Thackeray is but a distant memory.

This country is almost free from mill chimneys or industrial development. Instead there are many reminders of Armagh's more distant past. On the road from Portadown to Armagh you pass within a mile or so of the church of Kilmore from *An Chill Mhór* meaning, 'the Great church', referring to an ancient monastery which was located here. In an eighth-century document, *Feilire Aonghusa*, we are told that it was founded by St Mochta of Louth. It was believed that St Patrick also called here on his way to Armagh. The church was later dedicated to St Aidan, an early patron of Kilmore, who evangelised the northern part of England and founded the monastic church at Lindisfarne.

The ancient monastery of **Kilmore** belonged to the order of the *Céili Dé* or Culdees, which means, 'the servants of God'. Little is known of them except that they were bodies of disciples who attached themselves in a loose way to a holy man or sacred shrine. They formed themselves into monastic communities with settlements in Ireland, Scotland, and England. The ancient monastery was situated on the hill opposite the church where Kilmore House stands today. Well into the eighteenth century, walls and cells of the old monastery were visible and although no remains are evident today, they now form part of the fabric of Kilmore House. According to the *Ordnance Survey Memoirs*, 1837, 'There was a monastery near the church, the foundation of which was visible about 70 years ago, and the graveyard seems to have been of great extent, judging from the skeletons which have been found in the surrounding fields.'

Kilmore also had a holy well known as *Ciarán na nGort*. It was situated in the glebe land of the church which, in modern times, was also known as the 'Rector's Garden', but was anciently known as *Fearann an tSagairt* meaning, 'the priest's land'. It is opposite the old school house with an entrance through an archway. Ciarán, according to tradition, could have been a Welsh saint and his well was a place of pilgrimage until the sixteenth century.

Kilmore House.

Kilmore parish church.

Kilmore parish church was rebuilt in 1814 on a much older structure, which stands in the extensive graveyard surrounding the church on all sides. The church grounds offer a splendid view of the distant countryside with the great mound of Deirdre of the Sorrows prominent to the south-east. The square tower of the church has walls of immense thickness, which enclose a spiral staircase. The *Ordnance Survey Memoirs* described the church as 'a neat stone building', and the interior as having, 'a small gallery at the west end and a good organ. The windows are Gothic. The accommodation is for 700 persons and the general attendance is 500'.

The parish has not greatly changed since the *Ordnance Survey Memoirs* described it as, 'rich and of a home pleasing scenery, much improved by the rich appearance of the numerous orchards which abound throughout the parish'. John Hewitt, the Ulster poet who had a great influence on the work of Seamus Heaney and a later generation of Ulster poets, was drawn to Kilmore parish where his paternal grandparents had been born. He dubbed it the 'Townland of Peace':

> Once in a showery summer, sick of war,
> I strode the roads that slanted to Kilmore,
> That church-topped mound where half the tombstones wear,
> My people's name; some notion drew me there,
> Illogical, but not to be ignored,
> Some need of roots saluted, some sought word
> That might give me strength and sense to my slack rein,
> By this directed, not to lose again
> The line and compass so my head and heart
> No longer plunge and tug to drag apart.

To the east of the main road between Portadown and the city of Armagh stands the village of **Richhill**. The Sacheverell family were granted the Richhill district during the Plantation of Ulster. They built a castle in Mulladry, destroyed in 1641, and of which nothing now remains except an armorial stone brought to Richhill and placed in a house in the town. The present mansion was built in 1665 at what was then known as Legacorry, by Major Edward Richardson, who married the Sacheverell heiress. Legacorry, later became known as Richardson's Hill, and was subsequently shortened to Richhill.

The official name of the townland in which Richhill is situated remains Rich Hill

Richhill.

Above: Richhill.

Left: Richhill Castle.

or Legacorry, the latter name deriving from Irish *Log an Choire*, meaning hollow of the cauldron. The cauldron may refer to a pool in the Tall River, which bounds the townland on the east. Richhill's former importance was due partly to the fact that the main road from Armagh to Belfast went through it until the late seventeenth century, but, according to the *Ordnance Survey Memoirs* of 1837, 'the new line of road passes five-eighths of a mile north of it and is very well laid out. On it there are two coaches running daily from Armagh to Belfast through Portadown'.

Richhill became a Quaker stronghold in the seventeenth century. The Meeting House, built by public subscription in 1793, is located off Irish Street and is approached by a broad, walled, sloping avenue about 50 yards in length. Quakers were to play a major role in the development of the linen industry in the area, and a major market, established by Richardson in 1683, helped establish Richhill's early prosperity. According to the *Ordnance Survey Memoirs*:

> About 50 years ago there was an excellent market in this town, the best in the country for linen cloth, and it is even said that the inhabitants of Armagh came here to purchase their wearing apparel and victualling, which would imply a great superiority in this market over their own. The market, which is held on Saturday, is now merely nominal, not more than 40 persons attending it, and their only dealing is in yarn. This falling off in the market of Rich Hill is said to be owing to the hostility of the Quakers, who resolved to desert the town in consequence of one of their members having been killed in some riot in the place.

According to *Bassett's Guide* of 1888, the railway also had a major impact in the decline of the local market, 'After the opening of the railway between Armagh and Belfast, it [the linen market] began to decline as a market, and a great many hand-loom weavers moved away … Two tanneries and a preserve factory are the chief industries.' Evidence of Fruitfield, a Quaker-owned jam manufactory, is still conspicuous from the main Portadown-Armagh route by a tall red-brick chimney and extensive premises on raised ground.

On the other hand the railway brought many benefits. The heartland of Armagh's fruit-growing country is criss-crossed with abandoned railway lines which, until the closure of the Armagh-Portadown in 1957, were an important artery of the Great Northern line. The little station at Annaghmore owed its existence to the district's importance as an apple-growing area, and Richhill station also had a prominent fruit-export function, even though the station was one and a quarter miles from the village. Loughgall was served by a stopping-point named Retreat Halt, which had, no platform. Maps still show the route of the old railway line making its way south from Portadown to Armagh. T.G.F. Paterson, at the time the distinguished curator of Armagh Museum, recalled that final run from Armagh to Portadown in September 1957, when the station was crowded by local people who had come to say goodbye:

> Despite the fog signals and the excitement generally, it was a sad occasion. Photographers' flashlights blinked at us as we crowded into the train ... We soon reached the Retreat Halt where we found a crowd awaiting us and were held up for a considerable time. Eventually we moved onwards in a battery of cheers to Richhill Station where we found an even larger concourse of people awaiting us. There we were given a royal welcome and again, to the accompaniment of fog signals and more cheers, proceeded to Portadown. There we found a practically empty station. Evidently the inhabitants of the borough were quite uninterested in the fact that no more trains would pass through Portadown on their way to Armagh.

Back on the main A3 road, just three miles from Armagh is **Castledillon House**, which is of great architectural and historical interest. Turning down the Drumilly Road to the right past Hockley Lodge, once home to the Caulfield family and now a residential home, you will reach the entrance of Castledillon House in about one mile. Samuel Molyneux, chief engineer of Ireland, inherited the estate from the last of the Dillon family in the mid-seventeenth century and it remained in the Molyneux family until 1926. Coote described it in 1804, as, 'situated low and very old fashioned'. The *Ordnance Survey Memoir* for the 1830s was more impressed by the grounds than the buildings, 'The house stands in the centre of an extensive demesne containing a great deal of wood and ornamental plantation, with a large and picturesque lake which adds much to the beauty of the place.'

Sir George built the current house in 1845. It is a plain, austere, classical house

Castledillon.

Above left: Castle Dillon Obelisk.

Above right: Gate House, Loughgall *c.* 1990.

designed by William Murray, who was also the architect for St Luke's, the Armagh District Asylum. The eighteenth-century house remained until the new house was completed on the site of the original Dillon house and was then demolished. For many years it was used as a sanatorium by St Luke's Hospital, Armagh. Castledillon is now a private nursing home. It has a magnificent situation on a hill overlooking Castledillon lake, the land between being a large terraced lawn.

Close-by stands a 60-foot high obelisk, on a 12-foot high square base at the summit of Cannon Hill, with a black slab on the front, bearing the inscription, 'This Obelisk was erected by the Right Hon. Sir Capel Molyneux, of Castle Dillon, Bart in the year 1782, to commemorate the glorious revolution which took place in favour of the constitution of the kingdom, under the auspices of the volunteers of Ireland.'

Sir Capel Molyneux succeeded his brother, Daniel, to the title of Baronet and to all the estates, except Castle Dillon, which he did not inherit until 1759, when the former wife of his late first cousin died. An MP in the Irish House of Commons, he was a member of the Patriot movement, which sought greater independence for the Irish Parliament. In this they were supported by the Volunteer movement, a part-time military force raised in 1778 to meet the potential threat of French invasion. Shortly after its formation, the Volunteers adopted a more overtly political role as radical politicians took leading positions in the force. The Volunteers played an important role in the campaign for free trade and then led the drive for legislative independence. In 1782, the Irish Parliament was granted a large measure of independence, which ended only eighteen years later with the Act of Union.

For those wishing a more tranquil approach to Armagh, a network of roads run south-west from Portadown through Richhill, Kilmore, and Loughgall taking in a district covered with fruit trees and bushes, which are at their most spectacular in spring. Richard Hayward, the author of *In Praise of Ulster*, could write as recently as 1939, 'This is the district of gardens and orchards and thick-set damson hedges … It is all very beautiful, and very orderly, and very English, and the Warwickshire Planters certainly left their mark on this countryside as they left it on the vocabulary of the people.' Denis Hanna wrote in similar vein in the 1950s:

> It is a charming country in springtime, the little wave-like hills roll up and down, crested with the white and pink foam of apple and cherry blossom. Sometimes you round a corner to find your way almost barred by a laburnum or almond in flower, and beyond, the low thatch of the barn, so mellow with age and so much part of the ground from which it springs as to be scarcely discernable at first glance.

Apples have been grown in Britain and Ireland since the time of the Roman Empire. Legend has that the first apple tree in Ulster was planted at the ancient settlement of Ceangoba near Armagh by St Patrick himself. The first documented evidence, though, is not till 1156, when the obituary of the head of a local tribe praises him for the strong cider he brewed. By the seventeenth century most large houses in Co. Armagh had their own orchards. Two centuries later, there were over 100 apple varieties being grown in Ulster, with delightful names like Widow's Whelps, Irish Peach, Angel's Bites, and Strawberry Cheeks. Today more than 4,000 acres of Co. Armagh are covered in apple trees and it is thought that approximately 90 per cent of these crops are brambly apples, which are harvested here and then exported to the rest of the world. If you visit in May you can take the Apple Blossom Tours which take in the lovely orchards and old houses of Armagh, at a time when the hills are rich with apple blossom.

The centre of this district is **Loughgall,** a quaint old place more English than Irish in atmosphere. Loughgall stems from the Irish *Locha Cal* meaning, 'cabbage lake'. In the eighth century there was a settlement of the Culdees at Loughgall. Today it consists of one long street, which runs into a little valley and rises again. At the centre of the village is an enormous set of gates, which lead to Loughgall Manor. An imposing building, the Manor was once the residence of the Cope family, who arrived as part of the Plantation of Ulster in the seventeenth century. The Manor House was purchased by the Ministry of Agriculture in 1947 and is closed to the public. The grounds, however, consist of a 188-acre estate with an eighteen-hole golf course, coarse fishery, attractive walls, and cultivated wall garden are open to the public.

The Copes were an old established English family from Hanwell, Oxfordshire. In 1619, Pynnar made a survey of the Ulster plantation on behalf of the British Government and reported that a bawn – fortified farmhouse – had already been constructed:

> Mr. Cope has 3,000 acres called Derrycravy and Dromilly (in Co. Armagh). Upon this there is a bawn of lime and stone an hundred and eighty feet square, fourteen feet high with four flankers (defensive towers) and in three of them he has built very good lodgings which are three storeys high. There are also two water mills and one wind-mill and near to the bawn, he hath built fourteen houses of timber, which are inhabited with English families.

Loughgall Gate House, Manor House.

Above: Loughgall.

Right: Manor House,
Loughgall.

Old Loughgall church.

Sir Phelim O'Neill.

In 1641, the native Irish rebelled against the English and Scottish, and quickly overran and destroyed most of the settlements in Ulster. Loughgall remained intact until 1643, but in that year it was sacked and burned following a battle fought between the Scottish Army under General Monroe, and the Irish Army, commanded by Sir Phelim O'Neill and Owen Roe O'Neill. Following this battle many of the Loughgall plantation settlers were put to death and stories are told to this day of the English settlers being rounded up and locked in the church which was set on fire.

The eventual defeat of the Irish forces led to the restoration of the estates to the English and Scottish settlers in the region. Loughgall developed slowly under the benign guidance of the Cope family. The village took on a distinctly English appearance with fine Georgian houses, many of them coloured the pink of apple blossom. Although apple growing over the past two centuries has become a major factor in the economic development of Loughgall, the Cope family did not encourage the development of the brewing industry. The Copes went as far as buying several public houses in the village and closing them down. In their place they established a coffee house and reading room. According to *Bassett's Guide* in 1888:

A great many of the farmers are fruit growers, more or less extensively, and in the season of bloom the orchards contribute greatly to heighten the charm of the scenery. Mrs Cope, it appears, considered that the thirstiest mortal could find enjoyment in such a fair region without the aid of either brewer or distiller. She tested the truth of her opinion by purchasing the "vested right" of the village publicans, and setting up a coffee tavern as a substitute. To this she added a library and reading room. The nearest publican hangs out his sign at a distance of one mile from the village.

Visitors be warned there is no public house in the village of Loughgall to this day. Swift, who is best remembered for his associations with Markethill, was also on friendly terms with Robert Cope. Swift wrote:

> I am grown so peevish, that I can bear no other country-place in this Kingdom (than Loughgall); I quarrel everywhere else and sour the people I go to as well as myself … The worst of it is, that if you grow weary of me (and I wonder why you do not), I have no other retreat.

In a letter headed, 'Lough Gall July 22nd 1722' to Charles Ford of Woodford, Co. Meath, Swift paints an amusing picture of his host:

> I have been here three Weeks with your Old Friend Mr Cope, who is the most domestick man you ever saw, with a Wife whom he is so silly as to love, and who deserves it as well as a Wife can; and with nine Children, with whom he troubles himself as much and his Friends as little as possible. I have had little Benefit of Summer since I left Dublin, the continuall Rains have deprived me of riding and walking, and I believe the Clymate has not got much Credit with you. My Comfort is, that the People, the Churches and the Plantations made me think I am in England. I mean only the Scene of a few miles about me, for I passed through miserable Regions to get to it.

An anecdote about Swift survives from his period of his stay in Loughgall. One Sunday when he went to preach at Kilmore church, Swift arrived to find that the bell was silent although the hour of the service was near. On enquiring, he was told that the sexton was waiting for the sight of Mr Richardson's coach coming from Richhill. 'If', he declared, 'the bell of Kilmore hangs on the wheels of Mr. Richardson's carriage he can take the service himself', and he rode back to Loughgall. By October 1722, he was back in Dublin and writing to Robert Cope discussing ecclesiastical, social, and political affairs. He concluded, 'My most humble service to Mrs Cope, who entertained that covetous lampooning Dean much better than he deserved'.

Loughgall is also considered the birthplace of the Orange Order. It was in Jackson's house in Loughgall that the Constitution of the Loyal Orange Society was drawn up, and the table on which this took place is still preserved there. The museum occupies a terraced house at the northern end of the main street and includes Orange paraphernalia as sashes, flags, and the banner from the Dolly Brae victory. The distinguished Ulster poet, W.R. Rodgers who was Presbyterian minister of Cloveneden church and lived in Loughgall for twelve years before and after the Second World War, summed up the Ulster Protestant temperament:

> I am Ulster, my people an abrupt people
> Who like the spiky consonants in speech
> And think the soft ones cissy; who dig
> The k and t in orchestra, detect sin
> In sinfonia, get a kick out of
> Tin cans, fricatives, fornication, staccato talk,
> Anything that vies or takes attack,
> Like Micks, Tagues, tinkers' gets, Vatican.

The Battle of the Diamond, which resulted in the formation of the Orange Order, took place between Portadown and Loughgall in 21 September 1795. The battle was the result of a build-up of tension between the Protestant Peep o' Day Boys and the Roman Catholic Defenders. A farmer named Daniel Winter and his sons owned the field of action. During the battle, the property at the crossroads was attacked. Daniel Winter and his sons defended their property for as long as possible, having to retreat to the Diamond Hill when the thatch was fired. Local landowner, and a leading Orangeman, William Blacker left an account of the battle:

> At the time my father was adding to his dining room which occasioned the stripping
> of a considerable quantity of lead from the roof of the house. On the night of Thursday,
> the 17th, a carpenter's apprentice, Thomas Macan, and I made free with the best part of
> the lead and sat up nearly the entire night casting it into bullets of different sizes which
> Macan found means of having conveyed to our side the next day.

William Blacker recalled that the Peep o' Day took position on the brow of a hill overlooking The Diamond where:

with cool and steady aim at the swarms of Defenders, who were in a manner cooped up in the valley and presented an excellent mark for their shots. The affair was of brief duration … from the bodies found afterwards by the reapers in the cornfields, I am inclined to think that not less than thirty lost their lives.

Close to the site of the battle, Dan Winter's cottage is now open to the public. This old thatched cottage, which dates back to pre-1750, consists of living quarters, spirit grocers, and weavers' quarters with a full working loom. Its timbers still bear the scorch marks from when the house was set alight during the battle. At 94ft long it is believed to be the longest thatched cottage in Ireland. Still owned by the Winter family, visitors can see the room where these founding fathers met, and where there are to be seen old muskets and pikes, as well as an old sword found many years ago in the thatch.

Also outside Loughgall, but of much older vintage, is the ruin of an old Plantation brawn, known as **Castle Raw** or Castle Roe. Castle Raw was probably built in 1618 by Anthony Cope. The castle appears to have been a three-storey, fortified house in cruciform shape, built within a square entrenchment. Only the northern wall of the western wing now stands to approximately original height, the rest of the walling being largely reduced to foundations. According to the *Ordnance Survey Memoirs*, 1837, 'The country people have taken the greater part of it away to build houses'. It is hard to believe as one travels the narrow sloping road to the top of the hill, that Castle Roe has long been a tourist attraction. According to Bassett in 1888, 'John Cooke, a handloom weaver, rents a small house close to the castle, and takes pleasure in showing it to visitors.' Locals claimed that a structure existed here before the Plantation, according to both the *Ordnance Survey Memoirs* and *Lewis' Topographical Dictionary*. They later declared:

> In the townland of Castle Roe are extensive ruins of the castle which gave name to the district, and which is said to have been founded by Rory O'Nial in the reign of Elizabeth; it occupied a lofty eminence, commanding the entire country. The former glebe-house was part of the ancient abbey, and contained several dormitories and cells with narrow lights and very massive walls; but the only vestige of the abbey is the holy well, enclosed in the rector's garden. On a high hill in the parish, Cromwell is said to have had an encampment.

A further fives miles or so north from Loughgall, and only a few miles apart, are two National Trust properties worth visiting: Ardress House and The Aghory. **The Aghory**, situated on a wooded estate overlooking the Blackwater River,

Dan Winter's Cottage.

was built in 1824 for Walter McGeough. This superb neo-classical house, set in 315 acres, has maintained much of its original contents and structure, and houses four generations of family treasures. Its most notable feature is a cabinet barrel organ, built by James Bishop of London, which is still in working order. Also to be seen is the rare acetylene gas plant, installed in 1906, which for seven decades was used to light gas lamps in the house. There is a rose garden on the grounds, which contains a sundial bearing the inscription, 'Here reader mark the silent steps of never standing time.'

A few miles from the Aghory is **Ardress,** a charming gentleman farmer's residence. Originally a seventeenth-century house, it was enlarged with a series of extensions at various times between 1780 and 1810, all cleverly incorporated behind symmetrically composed façades. One of these additions includes a splendid drawing-room that could belong to a sophisticated Dublin town mansion of the period; above all else it gives Ardress its elegance and distinction. The central portion of Ardress, behind the five centre windows of the front facade, is a two-storey gable-ended house built sometime around 1670, for the Clarke family. In addition to upgrading the house, the Trust have restored the mainly eighteenth-century farmyard, where visitors can inspect a milking shed, dairy, boiler house, forge, and threshing barn. There is also an interesting display of old farm implements.

Above left: Castle Raw.

Above right: Ardress House.

A mile south-east at Aghory the Presbyterian church commemorates the father and son founders of the Disciples of Christ, an American fundamentalist church which now has over 1½ million adherents. Thomas Campbell had a small farm and bible teaching school here. He emigrated from Richhill to the Pennsylvanian backwoods, followed shortly afterwards by his son Alexander, known as the 'Sage of Bethany'. The tower and memorial window at Aghory were a gift from American church members.

If you continue to travel west along this road you will come to the villages of **Blackwatertown** and **Charlemont**, now of small importance, but in the time when the Earls of Tyrone disputed ownership of Armagh with the English, very important places indeed. The Blackwater River defines the border between counties Armagh and Tyrone. Blackwatertown was a very important station on the Ulster Canal. Warehouses and unusually big merchants' dwellings are all that remains of the village's industrial heyday. According to *Bassett's Guide* in 1888:

> Fifty years ago the population was almost three times greater than at present. The canal was not then finished. Blackwatertown was an important centre for the distribution of general merchandise. Vessels of 50 tons burden were able to navigate the Blackwater, and took from here large quantities of grain and potatoes.

Blackwatertown, or Portmore as it was then called, was the location for a strong fort built in 1575 by the Earl of Sussex to command the pass between Armagh and O'Neill territory to the west, and to facilitate later military excursions into Co. Tyrone. From Benburb almost opposite, and from their chief town of Dungannon, the O'Neills made frequent raids upon those parts of Armagh, which they had claimed as their own from immemorial times, and the Fort of Portmore was repeatedly attacked. In 1598, Hugh O'Neill, Earl of Tyrone, finally exasperated by the gradual penetration of his territories by the English, made a large-scale attack upon Portmore, and although the English Captain Williams defended his post bravely, he became so reduced by starvation and siege-weariness that he would have surrendered had not an army under Sir Henry Bagenal arrived.

Bagenal, with 300 horse and 4,000 foot, had reached Armagh without incident on 13 August. O'Neill had long prepared for his enemy's arrival. He was in command on the left, O'Donnell on the right, Randal MacDonnel close-by and Sir Hugh Maguire leading the force. According to the *Annals of the Four Masters*:

Above left: Earl of Charlemont.

Above right: Charlemont Fort Gate House.

When O'Neill had received intelligence that this great army was approaching him, he sent his messengers to O'Donnell, requesting of him to come to his assistance against this overwhelming force of foreigners who were coming to his country. O'Donnell proceeded immediately, with all his warriors, both infantry and cavalry, and a strong body of forces from Connaught, to assist his ally against those who were marching upon him. The Irish of all the province of Ulster also joined the same army, so that they were all prepared to meet the English before they arrived at Armagh.'

Besides the forces raised from the Ulster clans, O'Neill also had a substantial number of mercenaries in his pay, many of them from the Highlands of Scotland.

As soon as they left the Armagh garrison, the Crown Forces were all harassed with musket fire and spears thrown by rebel forces concealed in the woods. As a result, the different regiments became separated from one another as they paused to deal with hit-and-run attacks. O'Neill had also constructed a long trench running almost a mile between two bogs. Behind, a heavy saker stuck in the bed of a stream oozing out of a bog – the yellow ford which gave the battle its name. The regiment succeeded in crossing this trench, but then came under heavy attack from large forces and decided to retreat back behind the trench again. The regiment suffered significant losses during that retreat.

Henry Bagenal was killed by a shot through the head, which increased the sense of panic among the troops, and then their gun-powder store exploded, apparently ignited accidentally by the fuse of a matchlock musket. Seeing their enemy in confusion, the O'Neill cavalry rushed at the head of the forward part, followed by swordsmen on foot. Crown troops at the yellow ford were cut to pieces, and any wounded survivors left on the field after the battle were slain as well. The rest of the crown forces had to struggle their way back to the Armagh garrison. They reached it largely intact, but were harried all the way by the Irish.

Crown forces lost about 800 killed at the battle, together with 400 wounded, and some 300 deserting to O'Neill's side. Out of 4,000 soldiers who had set out from Armagh, just over 2,000 reached the town after the battle. After three days' negotiations, it was agreed that the crown troops could leave Armagh as long as they left their arms and ammunition behind them. They were evacuated by sea from Newry to Dublin. O'Neill's forces lost perhaps 200 to 300 in the battle, though sources for the number lost on O'Neill's side are very scanty. It was the greatest victory Gaelic Ulster ever achieved over the Crown. The exact site is still in dispute but seems to have been somewhere between the river and Grange church. A narrow lane beside this church is still known as, 'The Bloody Loanin', from the number of English fugitives who were slaughtered there as they fled before the victory-mad Irishmen.

The Irish forces proved incapable of consolidating this splendid victory and the Crown forces soon returned under Mountjoy to build a new and more formidable fortress at Charlemont. Prior to his founding of Charlemont Fort, the place had been called *Achad an Da Charadgh*, meaning 'the field of the two weirs', but it was renamed in his honour, using his name and the French word for hill, 'Mont'. In 1650, Charlemont was besieged by English Parliamentarian forces during the Cromwellian conquest of Ireland. The English took the fort from its Irish Catholic garrison under Phelim O'Neill, despite sustaining heavy casualties.

Charlemont Fort, Gate House.

Ironically, the fort would be destroyed almost three centuries later, during a new phase of conflict between the Crown forces and its Irish enemies. Inside the fort was a seventeenth-century governor's house, which resembled one of those hunting lodges built in the castle style in Elizabethan or Jacobean England, with symmetrical bows and clusters of chimneys rising like turrets from its four corners. It remained a government building until 1858, when it was acquired by the Charlemont family. James Caulfield, 1st Earl of Charlemont, famous as the 'Volunteer' Earl of Charlemont, lived mostly at Charlemont House and at Marino, the seat which he acquired just outside Dublin. However they seemed to be more concerned with looking after their large house, Roxborough Castle, just on the other side of the River Blackwater. The central building of Charlemont Fort was attacked and burned by a body of armed men on 30 July 1920, by which time it was occupied only by a caretaker. The ruins were bought by a contractor who sold the bricks and stones for cheap building material. The surviving gatehouse probably dates from the late seventeenth century but it was extensively restored in the eighteenth century.

Chapter 5

South from Tandragee

Five miles south-east of Portadown along the A27 is the town of Tandragee from the Irish *Tóin re Gaoith*, 'backside to the wind'. It is worth stopping half way along this route to enjoy Brackagh Moss, an extensive peat-land trail, nestling in a small tributary valley adjoining the Cusher and Bann Rivers. The Belfast–Dublin railway line passes close-by, and was the location of a railway disaster in 1886. Six people were killed and forty injured when, as a result of the neglect of the permanent way, the track gave way and the train ran off the line.

The town of **Tandragee** is a much older settlement than either Lurgan or Portadown. It owes its origins to the O'Hanlons who dominated the region from the thirteenth century and it was they who built a castle where the present Tandragee Castle now stands. During the Plantation of Ulster the lands passed into the hands of Sir Oliver St John from Lydiard Tregoze in Wiltshire. By 1622, he had rebuilt the castle and a 'pleasant park', a 'handsome' church, and a village of twenty-seven houses 'well built of the English fashion, making a fair large street'.

The O'Hanlons attacked and burned the castle in the 1641 Rising. Sir Oliver St John was shot through the head while directing the defence of the castle. Although the St John family were restored to their lands, the O'Hanlon's continued to haunt them in the form of the highwayman, Redmond O'Hanlon. Born in 1640 near Pontzpass, O'Hanlon began as a footboy to Sir George Acheson of Markethill, and, after a brief period of employment as a poll tax collector, he joined a band of tories, from the Irish word *tóraidhe,* meaning 'pursued man', led by his kinsman, Laughlin O'Hanlon. Imprisoned for stealing horses, he bribed his way out of Armagh gaol. By 1674, the colonial authorities in Dublin had put a price of £10 on his head, with posters advertising for his capture, dead or alive. O'Hanlon was wounded in a close encounter with a force hired to track him down, and had, to lie up for a time on Ram's Island on Lough Neagh. He returned to continue his activities in south Armagh and even as far north as Tandragee itself. On 9 September 1679, Henry St John was riding on his estate with a manservant and the Revd Lawrence Power, the Church of Ireland Rector of Tandragee. A party of O'Hanlon's associates came upon the group at Knockbridge near Tandragee, and killed St John, shooting him twice in the head.

At the landlord's funeral, an outraged Revd Power denounced the rapparees and those landowners who did business with them. The full text of his sermon was subsequently printed in London under the name, *The Righteous Man's Portion.* James Butler, 1st Duke of Ormonde, Lord Deputy of Ireland, ordered the assassination of Redmond O'Hanlon. He was murdered in his sleep by his foster brother and close associate Art MacCall O'Hanlon at Eight Mile Bridge near Hilltown, Co. Down on 25 April 1681. Art received a full pardon and £200 from the Duke of Ormond for murdering his leader. According to local tradition O'Hanlon is buried at Relicarn, an ancient graveyard on the road from Tandragee to Scarva. This burial ground is also notable because of an ecclesiastical bell found here, the earliest datable example of its kind yet discovered in Ireland.

During the late eighteenth century, Tandragee became a stronghold of the Orange Order, which was sweeping the county after the battle of the Diamond. An amusing anecdote was recorded by a French traveller who visited the area in 1798:

> On the way to Armagh I passed through a superb country; there is a charming valley, and well-wooded, near Tandragee. Between this town and Armagh I met a company of Orangemen, as they are called, wearing the orange cockades, and some of them having ties of the same colour. The peasantry seemed very much afraid of them. I went into one or two cabins to rest myself, and was offered, certainly, hospitality in the ordinary way, but it did not seem to be with the same air as before, and at last, near the town, a good woman said to me, "You seem to have come from far, my dear Sir, I hope that your umbrella or the string of it will not bring you into trouble". I laughed at the good woman's fears, but, on reflection, I felt that since she had remarked that my umbrella was greenish, and the cord of a bright green, soldiers might make the same observation, and that in any case it would be very disagreeable to have any trouble over such a silly thing, and I cut the green cord off my umbrella.

By the early nineteenth century, Tandragee had developed into a flourishing town helped by cheap transport supplied by the Newry canal. According to Sir Charles Coote in 1804:

Its contiguity to the Newry canal is no less favourable, which flows within a mile of the environs, and affords it all the advantages of trade with that commercial town, and also with Belfast; and the lands of this vicinity have, by the same conveyance, the benefit of procuring abundance of limestone, on easy terms, which so powerfully fertilizes the soil. The country around is thickly inhabited by wealthy bleachers; and the small farmers, who are very comfortable, are all engaged in the linen manufacture, so that it became no difficult matter to have a market established in Tandragee, which was soon numerously resorted to; insomuch that, at some times, the weekly sales of linens have amounted to the enormous sum of 7000.

For nearly two centuries, the castle remained a ruin after being burnt down during the rebellion of 1641. It was finally rebuilt in 1836 by the Duke of Manchester and has, ever since, been Tandragee's most notable building. The Castle was described in the *Ordnance Survey Memoirs* of 1838, while work on its reconstruction was still ongoing:

> Tandragee Castle, the residence of Lord Viscount Mandeville and Lady Mandeville, is a fine large stone building of the Elizabethan style of architecture, enclosing a good court…It contains a large handsome chapel, wainscoted with richly carved oak and it will also have an organ and gallery. The house contains large and commodious apartments, also a very valuable collection of theological works consisting of the old English and French divines collected by Lord Mandeville…It is built on the site of the former one and in making the improvements about the house a quantity of human skulls and bones have, at different times, been found by the workmen. Attached to the house is a good garden and conservatories, also a fine demesne, well planted and tastefully laid out.

J.B. Doyle, who toured Ulster in the early 1850s, was impressed by the fact that the 'grounds are generously thrown open by the noble proprietor, and form a delightful place for relaxation to the respectable inhabitants of the town'.

The castle remained the seat of the Dukedom in Ireland until 1939, when it was requisitioned by US troops who were housed there until the end of the war. The castle was not restored afterwards, and it was purchased in 1955 by the Hutchinson family who established the successful Tayto crisp business on the premises. Tayto is today one of the country's most successful snack-food businesses and regular tours are conducted of the factory during which visitors get the chance to see how the crisps and snacks are made, as well as getting a closer look at the Castle.

Leabharlanna Poibli Chathair Bhaile Átha Cliath
Dublin City Public Libraries

Tandragee is also home to one of Northern Ireland's premier golf courses. In 1911, the 9th Duke of Manchester, brought Mr John Stone, an eminent Scottish professional from Sandy Lodge Golf Club in London, to lay out a private golf course on his estate in Tandragee. The Duchess of Manchester, who was born in Cincinnati, Ohio, even designed some of the original bunkers, which were laid out in the shape of the Great Lakes, and these remain to this day. The course was subsequently leased to Tandragee golf club for many years, until 1975, when it was finally purchased from the Duke of Manchester's Estate. Few courses in Northern Ireland present golfers with such beautiful scenery and fine views, including that of the castle.

Apart from the castle, St Mark's church is Tandragee's other notable landmark. Built by Sir Oliver St John, it was rebuilt in 1684 and 1812. The influence of the Duke of Manchester is very apparent inside the church. The oak reredos which beautifies the chancel was formerly an integral part of the Duke's private chapel within the castle. So also were two carved cherubs which enhance the baptistery area near the entrance doors. When the parish church was being restored in 1812, the skull of Sir Oliver St John, indentified by means of the bullet-hole, was found. In 1849, transepts were added to the church, and on that occasion the skull was again exposed to view. It was stolen, but four days later was found in the churchyard wrapped in brown paper. In his *Armagh Directory*, Bassett recounts another story featuring the vault, told by carpenter Thomas Best to the local sexton, which is still remembered in the town to this day:

> He said that on opening the St John vault he saw an erect object resembling the form of a woman. It crumbled to dust on being touched with his rule. The supposed sudden death of a lady, who came on a visit to Tandragee a long time ago, is associated with the discovery by the carpenter. Interment was made in the St. John vault; in accounting for the erect object many persons were led to believe that she was buried alive, and on returning to consciousness was literally frozen to the spot near the door.

Before travelling south to Newry, it is worth taking a slight detour to the beautifully-situated village of Clare on the Cusher, a fine trout river. It is chiefly notable for being the site of the Earl of Bath's mill, which in 1641, was used as a prison by Sir Phelim O'Neill, the rebel leader. The nearby Clare Glen is an ideal location for those seeking a relaxing afternoon. The park is located within a winding river valley in an area of considerable natural beauty, enhanced by mature trees bordering the River Cusher.

Above:
Tandragee.

Left: St Marks'
church,
Tandragee.

On the way out of Tandragee the River Cusher flows under the eighteenth-century, four-arch bridge towards the extensive riverside premises of Thomas Sinton & Co. linen and yarn manufacturers. A few hundred yards upstream White's large red-brick flour mill straddles both sides of the approach to the town. The A27 from Tandragee to Newry takes the traveller through some of the most beautiful countryside in the county, and the effect is enhanced by the fact that for long stretches it runs parallel to the Newry Canal and the Belfast–Dublin railway line.

A few miles south of Tandragee along the A27, is the village of **Poyntzpass**, which has a long and troubled history. It was one of the three ancient passes into the county, and was given its name in recognition of Lieutenant Charles Poyntz's spirited defence of the region against a larger body of Irish troops in 1598. Sir Charles' son, Sir Toby Poyntz, in 1684, built a church at Acton nearby, and was buried in the chancel. This church is now in ruins but the village of **Acton**, named after his native village in England, founded by Sir Toby Poyntz, remains. Sir Toby built a bawn and twenty-four cottages for a group of English settlers. A petition that Sir Toby Poyntz submitted to government about 1662, contains evidence about problems caused to his tenants and himself by the estate's location on an important crossing place on the Glan Bog, that separated Co. Armagh from neighbouring Co. Down:

> the highway leading from the County of Armagh to the County of Down upon the river of the Gline commonly known by the name of Staroagh and Points his pass is a madeway of a causeway and timber bridge, and every year out of repair by reason of several droves of cattle, which every summer are driven over there to the great prejudice of the petitioner and the said tenants both in destroying their pastures and breaking down the said bridge and causeway and therefore humbly praying for an order empowering them to demand and receive moderate customs for every herd of cattle passing that way towards the repair of the said bridge and causeway, the petitioners obliging themselves to keep them in good repair.

Poyntzpass village itself dates only from the end of the eighteenth century when Thomas Alexander Steward, a direct descendant of Sir Charles Poyntz, established a village here. He called it Poyntzpass, the name by which the area had long been known. Stewart gave land for the building of churches and schools, and obtained for the village the right to hold fairs and markets. The Church of Ireland church, built in 1789, occupies the highest point in the village which expanded gently southwards to meet up with the church. It replaced the church at Acton and was erected in 1798 but not consecrated until 1822. Unusually, directly opposite the Church of Ireland church is that of the Church of the Redeemer.

Poyntzpass.

At Poyntzpass a castle, the remnants of which were visible until the middle of the nineteenth century, guarded the 'pass' in earlier times. Today, there is no trace of it other than in 'Castle Corner', the name by which a corner of William Street is sometimes known. However, the remains of a windmill stand prominently on the high ground to the west of the village. The strength of the walls and the narrow openings above the two entrances, gave rise to the view that this structure might originally have been a castle built by Poyntz to defend 'The Pass'. 'The Pass' was still thought to have a certain strategic significance up until the Second World War, when a concrete 'pill-box' or machine-gun post was constructed overlooking the bridge, as a potentially important crossing place in the event of invasion.

Close to Poyntzpass are **Tyrone's Ditches**, the remains of an earthwork thrown up by Hugh O'Neill, Earl of Tyrone, in his wars with Queen Elizabeth between 1594 and 1603. Near Poyntzpass, too, there are the remains of the **Black Pig's Dyke**, more commonly known in Co. Armagh as the **Danes' Cast**, a great travelling earthwork, linking up the portions in Scarva and Goraghwood, with the sections in Seafin and Aghayollogue. The Black Pig is explained in local legend as a wicked schoolmaster who was transformed into a pig and banished; the pig created the ditches with its snout as it rampaged angrily across the countryside. Scholars have suggested that it was a defensive line that stretched from Dundalk in Co. Louth, to Bundoran in Co. Donegal. The different sections of the separate dykes, however, date from different periods, leading to speculation that they may have marked boundaries of individual communities and may have had legal or religious purposes. The best preserved of these dykes in Ulster average about 30 feet wide and are still some 15 feet deep in places. The most perfect section now remaining is in Scarva Demesne close to Pontzpass.

Brownlow House Vault, Shankill, Lurgan.

Admiral David Lucas V.C., the first Ulsterman to win the Victoria Cross, was born at Drominargle, near Poyntzpass. During the Crimean War, Lucas was serving as a mate on the HMS *Hecla* which formed part of the fleet under the command of Admiral Sir Charles Napier. Stung by public criticism of their lack of success against the Russian fleet, the British fleet had been forced to attack the heavily defended shore forts where the Russian navy had been content to shelter.

The *Hecla*, and two sixteen-gun paddle-steamers under the Command of Captain W.H. Hall, attacked the coastal fortress of Bomarsund on the Aland Islands in the Baltic Sea. The ships came under fire from the batteries, and from Russian riflemen and artillery on the shore. All three ships anchored at about 9p.m. and bombarded the fortress until 1a.m. the next morning. At the height of the bombardment, a live shell from an enemy battery landed on *Hecla*'s upper-deck, with its fuse still hissing. All hands were ordered to fling themselves flat on the deck, but, according to Captain Hall, his commanding officer, Lucas, with 'a remarkable instance of coolness and presence of mind in action', ran forward and hurled the shell into the sea, where it exploded with a tremendous roar before it hit the water. Some minor damage was done to the ship's side and two men were slightly hurt, but, thanks to

Lucas, nobody was killed or seriously wounded. Lucas died at Great Culverden, Kent, on 7 August 1914, a few days after the outbreak of the First World War. His Victoria Cross can be seen at the National Maritime Museum at Greenwich.

West of Pontzpass is the village of **Mountnorris**, which takes its name from the fort erected here by John Norris in early Plantation times, to link up the Moyry Castle with Blackwatertown and Charlemont Forts. The area took its name by combining the names of Mountjoy and his campaign commander in the Low Countries, Sir John Norris. In 1600, Lord Mountjoy built an earthwork fort and left a garrison of 400 men under the command of Captain Edward Blaney in Mountnorris. Tyrone's men attempted to stop them as Mountjoy's secretary Fynes Moryson records:

> There began between our Foot and theirs, a very good Skirmish, till our Men did beat them off, and brought with them great Store of Corn and Wood, and killed divers of them. The next Day we began to work, in the building of the Fort, and to impeach our Work, the Rogues began to skirmish with us on both Sides, which was excellently maintained by some of few of our Men that we sent out. We saw many of them killed, and after understood they lost a great Number, whereof many were Horsemen, of the best sort, that had lighted to encourage their Men to fight.

By 1620, the village no longer had a garrison, and in the eighteenth century it passed into the hands of the Cope family of Loughgall, to become a rural settlement with no military connections. The village was originally intended to be the site of the Royal School but, due to instability at the time in Ulster, the school was resituated to its current site in Armagh and was opened in 1608.

Heading south from Poyntzpass it is worth taking a short detour to the village of Bessbrook, which is just three miles from Newry. Situated in a valley between Keggal Mountain and Slieve Gullion, the 'Model Village' of **Bessbrook** was founded in 1759 by John Pollock, a linen merchant. However, it was the Richardson family who imposed their Quaker outlook on the village, providing free medicine and non-sectarian education to its inhabitants. Planned on the lines of a William Penn settlement, the village represents an experiment in social reform begun in 1845, by John Grubb Richardson. High-quality houses were built but it was the absence of a police station, public house, or pawn shop which aroused the curiosity of visitors.

George Bernard Shaw visited Bessbrook in 1879, commenting that, 'Bessbrook is a model village where the inhabitants never swear nor get drunk and look as if they would very much like to do both'.

At one time, Bessbrook linen was among the finest in the world, and the linen mill provided most of the employment in the village. The mill was extended from time to time and the village grew with it. According to *Bassett's Guide* in 1888 one spinning mill alone had:

> 22,000 spindles, and one weaving factory from 500 to 660 looms. A hand-loom weaving factory occupies the spot where the Pollock wollen mill stood. Here the methods of "the good old days" for the production of superfine linens are still preserved. A green for yarn-bleaching by a particular process is also maintained. Works of the Company, in addition to those mentioned, extend for over a mile along the River Bess, between Camlough and Newry.

Each house built for the workers in Bessbrook originally had an allotment garden for the growing of vegetables. The area of the village where these were situated is still known as 'The Gardens', although the allotments themselves have been replaced by further housing. The interest the Richardson family took in the development of the village was underlined in *Bassett's Guide*:

> Each house has a garden containing an eighth of an acre, and when the tenant enters into possession he is required to sign an agreement which contains certain stipulations in regard to the keeping of fowl and pigs, so that they may not be found in the quarters occupied by the family or in the yard. He can have a pig-sty and fowl-run in the garden if he pleases. Another binding clause places him under obligation to send his children to school until they are old enough for mill-work.

It was decided to build a tramway to transport workers, and raw and finished materials, to and from these mills. This tramway, the second hydro-electric tramway in Ireland, was opened in 1885. It ran from the edge of Bessbrook to the edge of Newry. By an ingenious arrangement of the rails, the goods wagons, which had flangeless wheels, could be made to run on either road or rail, and so it was not necessary to build a line through Newry. The tramway remained in operation until 1948. One of the locomotives is preserved in The Ulster Folk & Transport Museum at Cultra Co. Down and a brake van is used in a local convent as a summer house.

It is said that Bessbrook was the inspiration for Cadbury Brother's Model Village of Bournville. The textile business continued until 1972, as The Bessbrook Spinning Company finally closed in 1987, and the main building was used as an Army Base until 2nd July 2007. It is currently empty.

Close to Bessbrook is **Derrymore House**, a picturesque thatched residence,

Above left: Admiral David Lucas VC.

Above right: Bessbrook Mill.

Right: Derrymore House.

where the Act of Union was drawn up in 1800. The house was constructed between 1776 and 1787, by Sir Isaac Corry on land he inherited from his father. The house, built in the cottage style, and the surrounding parkland was laid out by John Sutherland, one of the most celebrated disciples of Capability Brown. Sir Charles Coote was impressed by the house and grounds when he visited them at the beginning of the nineteenth century:

> The very fine improvements of Derrymore show the correct and elegant taste of Mr Southerland, who planned them, and superintended their execution...The young plantations already display a fine appearance of wood; the approaches are extremely well planned, and the cottage, which is as yet the only residence, is without exception, the most elegant summer lodge I have ever seen.

Although Sir Isaac Corry was to become Chancellor of the Irish Exchequer, he lacked the funds to build himself a more substantial dwelling. In his early years he was an active patriot and Irish Volunteer, but eventually earned the undying hostility of many of his former comrades by supporting the Act of Union, in alliance with his old schoolmate from Armagh Royal School, Lord Castlereagh. The debates in the Irish House of Commons got so heated that Henry Grattan challenged him to a duel and subsequently wounded him. After the abolition of the Irish parliament he drifted into obscurity, and sold Derrymore in 1810. By that time, the voters of Newry had turned against him and when the promised Catholic emancipation was not delivered, Corry had a road built, that led straight from the Dublin Road to his house, thus avoiding the town completely. This is still called the Chancellor's Road. Derrymore House was eventually acquired by the Richardson family who later donated the House and the estate at Bessbrook to the National Trust. It is now open to the public and visitors can enjoy a fine example of a charming eighteenth-century thatched cottage and beautifully-landscaped demesne.

Chapter 6

Armagh City

Armagh may be the smallest city in Ireland, with a population of 12,000, but take a look at a map of Co. Armagh, either old or modern, and it shows that Armagh City is at the centre of a great labyrinth of roads, underlining its centuries-old importance as a spiritual, administrative and military capital. Whichever road you take to the city of Armagh today, you are left in no doubt that it is a place with a distinguished pedigree. Denis Hanna, in his book *The Face of Ulster*, declared:

> As you near Armagh city you are conscious of approaching a focal point. Even if you should not know its ancient history, the handsome Georgian houses and demesnes that fan out round it would help you to guess that this area has held an important place in the national life for centuries.

This view echoed the opinion of the legendary travel writer, H.V. Morton, who visited Armagh in the 1930s:

> As it was growing dusk I entered Armagh, a city of red marble. Romance will always linger in the quiet streets of Ireland's Canterbury, for although there is little about to-day to remind one of ancient times its fame is not written in stone but in the history of faith and learning.

Although Armagh has always been referred to as a city, city status was only officially conferred by the Queen in 1995. Armagh has, nevertheless, been the spiritual capital of Ireland for over 1,500 years, and today is the seat of both the Anglican and the Roman Catholic archbishops of Ireland. In a county where most towns were established during the Plantation, Armagh's ancient pedigree is borne out by its street names some dating back 1,500 years. While side streets twist and curve up the steep hill to where the Cathedral of St Patrick has stood since the day when the saint made the city the Capital of his Church. But the site now occupied by Armagh was sacred long before the arrival of Christianity as testified by the mythical origins of its name. It was founded by a pagan queen named Macha and from her the city takes its name. Its centre was the hill on which the Church of Ireland Cathedral stands, which was then named *Ard Mhacha* or 'Macha's Height'. Today steep streets, climbing and intersecting, follow the curve of the ditches and bank, which ringed the rath and its church. As W.R. Rodgers so memorably described it:

> There is a through-otherness about Armagh
> Of tower and steeple,
> Up on the hill are the arguing graves of the king's
> And below are the people.

After some three centuries, the hill was abandoned in favour of Navan Fort about three miles to the west. In the fourth century AD, the King of Ulster was defeated, and Navan Fort abandoned. The new rulers returned to the present site of Armagh and it was here that St Patrick arrived in his mission to convert the Irish to Christianity. We know very few verifiable facts about the saint's life. What we do know can be traced to five documents, a *Confessio* and 'Epistle to Coroticus', attributed to him and thought reliable, and three memoirs/biographies written long after his death, that of Muirchu, Tirechan (both seventh century), and the anonymous *Bethu Phatraic* or *Vita Tripartita* (late eighth century) which draws on the first two texts and adds much material. None of these allow us to date St Patrick's mission with certainty, but the second half of the fifth century is now favoured. According to the *Confessio*, Patrick was a native of Roman Britain, the son of Calpurnius. His original Celtic name is alleged to have been Succat. Captured by Irish raiders, at the age of sixteen, he was sold into bondage to herd pigs and sheep for a chief named Milchu. Eventually, he escaped and returned home to Britain. He does not say where he was trained, but tradition suggests he was the disciple of St Germanus of Auxerre. Later chosen to be bishop, he returned to Ireland to become 'a slave for Christ'. In his own words, during a thirty-year mission he 'baptised thousands, ordained clerics everywhere and rejoiced to see the flock of the Lord in Ireland growing splendidly'.

In a country devoid of towns and cities in the European sense, he chose Armagh as his see. Roman districts of Britain were early organized into sees, and

Patrick, who was proud of his Roman citizenship, would naturally endeavour to establish in the country of his adoption the orderly system to which he had been accustomed at home and abroad. In accordance with this desire he founded the earliest bishopric in Ireland, that of Armagh: the first, and for the next 650 years the only fixed episcopal see in Ireland. For centuries after St Patrick's death, bishops in Ireland did not occupy fixed sees, and the country was not laid out in dioceses. They exercised their episcopal functions within the monasteries in a position subordinate to the abbot. Even Armagh did not long retain its metropolitan character and was unable to resist the pressure of native custom. It fell into line with the other Christian settlements and became primarily a monastic centre. It was not until the twelfth century that the archbishopric of Armagh was restored.

A major factor in Armagh's importance during the dark ages was the foundation by St Patrick of the monastery of St Peter and St Paul. It was later rebuilt by Imar O'Hoedegan, and was the most distinguished of the religious establishments which existed here, having materially contributed to the early importance of the place. The school of Armagh that grew up beside the monastery was one of the most celebrated in the Ireland of the sixth century. It attracted scholars from every part of Europe. One such was Aldfrid, later King of the Northumbrian Saxons, who remembered his time in Armagh fondly:

I found in Armagh the splendid
Meekness, wisdom and prudence blended
Fasting as Christ hath recommended
And noble councillors untranscended.

One part of the city was called Trian-Saxon, the Saxon's Third, from the number of Saxon students who lived there. The *Book of Armagh* was written in the monastery in A.D. 807. It is a copy of the New Testament in Latin, and bound up with it is the *Confessio* of St Patrick. At the end of the Confession the scribe Ferdomnach wrote, 'Thus far the volume which Patrick wrote with his own hand'. This was written three centuries after the saint's death and suggests that Ferdomnach was copying a manuscript – now, sadly lost – in St Patrick's writing. *The Book of Armagh* is now in Trinity College, Dublin, where you will see a well-thumbed page at the end, with an entry dated AD 1004, stating that the great King Brian Buru on his triumphal journey through Ireland visited Armagh, made an offering of gold on the altar of St Patrick, and confirmed the city in its ancient religious supremacy.

Market Street, Portadown.

It is said that 7,000 students were congregated in it, in the pursuit of learning; at one period; and the *Annals of Ulster* relate that, at a synod held by Gelasius at Claonadh in 1162, it was decreed that no person should lecture publicly on theology, except such as had studied at Armagh. It was its reputation as a centre of learning that earned Armagh the title of the City of Saints and Scholars. This institution received numerous grants of endowment from the native kings, the last of whom, Roderick O'Connor, made a grant to its professors in 1169.

The city was destroyed by fire during the seventh and eighth centuries, and suffered severely and repeatedly from the Viking attack in the ninth century as the raiders were attracted by the wealth of the monastic foundations. At last in 1014, the celebrated High King of Ireland, Brian Boru, broke the Viking's power at the Battle of Clontarf. The centuries which followed were no more peaceful however, with tribal warfare as the O'Neill's established their dominance over the area, and the invasion of Ulster by the Anglo-Normans in the twelfth century. The city also suffered severely from the invasion of Edward Bruce in 1315, during which the entire region was wasted, and the archbishop was reduced to a state of extreme destitution, by the reiterated incursions of the Scottish army.

During the local wars in Ulster, at the close of the fifteenth century and the beginning of the sixteenth century, the city was reduced to a state of great wretchedness. The Reformation caused further conflict and the last of the subsequent dissolution of the monasteries led to the dispersal of the monks from the city. Stones from the abbey of St Peter and Paul were later used for the Presbyterian church built in 1722, lower down Abbey Street. According to local tradition, in 1722 Dean Jonathan Swift was going up to the Cathedral in Armagh when he saw masons at work building the new Presbyterian meeting house in Abbey Street. He noted that they were re-using the carved stones from the ruined Abbey of Saint Peter and Paul, and that, 'these lunatic Puritans are chiselling the very Popery out of the stones.' Another tale about this incident recounts that the Dean quizzed the masons about their pay. On being told that it was a shilling a day, he commented that a good mason could be had in Dublin for nine pence, only to receive the riposte that in Armagh, 'we get a good Dean for £200 a year'. During work on the building in 1966, the original window openings were revealed, and from one on the east side, two carved pilaster heads dating from the fourteenth were recovered. One is ornamented with a pair of dolphins and the other with two birds, but they had been damaged when they were being reworked.

The Nine Years' War at the end of the sixteenth century once again reduced the city to poverty. Sir Arthur Chichester, Fynes Moryson, records, 'destroyed the rebels corn about Armagh (whereof he found great abundance) and would destroy the rest, this course causing famine, being the only sure way to reduce or root out the rebels.' By the beginning of the seventeenth century, therefore, the fortunes of Armagh were at a very low ebb. Thomas Blennerhasset visited in 1610, and commented:

> How exceedingly well standeth Armagh, better seat for rich soil there cannot be, but so poor, as I verily think all the household stuff in that city is not worth twenty pounds, yet it is the Primate of all Ireland, and as they say for antiquity one of the most ancient in all Europe: it is also of so small power as forty resolute men may rob, rifle and burn it: were it a defended corporation it would soon be rich and religious, and the security would make one acre more worth than now twenty be.

His judgement is confirmed by Richard Bartlett's map a few years earlier, which shows devastated ecclesiastical buildings with the comment, 'Armagh hath lost all its ancient beauty and grandeur and nothing remaineth but a few wattled cottages with the ruinous walls of the monasterie, priorie and Primat's pallace'.

Armagh was then garrisoned with English troops, but following the Flight of the Earls in 1607, when the Early of Tyrone along with his family, retainers, and fellow lords, fled to the Continent, their lands were seized by the Crown, and in January 1608 a plan, which called for the plantation of much of Ulster, was published. A grant of July 1620, vested Sir Toby Caulfield, master of the Ordnance, 'the abbey or monastery of the Apostles Peter and Paul, of house of canons of Saint Augustine's Order, at Armagh, with the site thereof, and buildings thereon, the cemetery, garden and orchard on the east side thereof, extending ...'

A large number of Scottish settlers subsequently settled in and around the city of Armagh. At the commencement of the war in 1641, Armagh fell into the hands of Sir

Phelim O'Nial, who, on being soon after forced to evacuate it, set fire to the Cathedral, and put to death many of the inhabitants. The city also changed hands several times during the Williamite Wars. When James II, in his progress through the north to and from the siege of Derry, rested for a few days at Armagh, he described as having been pillaged by the enemy, and very inconvenienced both for himself and his suite.

It was with considerable justification therefore that Dr William Reeves, Dean of Armagh and librarian at Armagh in the 1850s, wrote:

> No city is so rich in historical associations, and yet has so little to show, and so little to tell in the present day, as Armagh. St. Patrick's first church is now represented by the Bank of Ireland; the Provincial Bank comes close on St. Columba's; St. Bride's shares its honours with a paddock; St. Peter and St. Paul afford stabling to a modern rus in urbe; and St. Mary's is lost in a dwelling-house.

It was the arrival of Archbishop Richard Robinson that was to change Armagh's fortunes, and his audacious building programme has given the city some of its finest buildings. Richard Robinson was born in Yorkshire and came to Ireland as chaplain to the Duke of Dorset. In 1765, he was made Archbishop of Armagh and Primate of All Ireland, and in 1777, Baron Rokeby. Significantly, he decided to live in the city, unlike many of his predecessors who had preferred the relative comfort and safety of Co. Louth, or in Dublin. According to James Boswell, Robinson's sermons were 'excellent in style and doctrine, though his voice was low'. The memoirist, Richard Cumberland, who knew him well, said Robinson was, 'publickly ambitious of great deeds and privately capable of good ones', and that he, 'supported the first station in the Irish hierarchy with all the magnificence of a prince palatine', despite a small private fortune.

Richard Robinson built himself a palace in Armagh, was responsible for the construction of the public library, and, in 1789, built the observatory at his own expense. He also compelled his tenants to rebuild their houses in stone and slate as their leases fell in. This was a relatively simple matter for the archbishop, since existing leases on bishops' land lapsed on the arrival of a new incumbent. Arthur Young visited the city and met with Primate Robinson in 1776:

> His Grace rode out with me to Armagh, and showed me some of the noble and spirited works by which he has perfectly changed the face of the neighbourhood. The buildings he has erected in seven years, one would suppose, without previous information, to be the work of an active life.' He found it a nest of mud cabin, and he will leave it a well-built city of stone and slate.

Above left: Archbishop Robinson.

Above centre: Armagh old St Patrick's Church of Ireland Cathedral.

Above right: Armagh St Patrick's Roman Catholic Cathedral.

Lord John Beresford, who became primate in 1822, also made major contributions to the development of the city. He made considerable additions to the palace, the library and the Royal School and it was during his administration that the Church of Ireland Cathedral was extensively restored. William Makepeace Thackeray visited Armagh during Beresford's episcopacy, and later wrote:

> The greater part of Armagh has the aspect of a good stout old English town, although round about the steep on which the cathedral stands (the Roman Catholics have taken possession of another hill, and are building an opposition cathedral on this eminence) there are some decidedly Irish streets, and that dismal combination of house and pigsty which is so common in Munster and Connaught.

The Episcopal **Cathedral of Armagh** stands on the site where, in 445, St Patrick built his first church. According to Muirchu's, *Life of Patrick*, the saint was not given the top of the hill as he had requested, but lower down in what is now Scotch Street, currently the site of the Bank of Ireland. Some time later the chieftain grazed his horse on Patrick's land, which displeased him greatly because, he said, Daire 'has behaved foolishly in sending brute animals to disturb the small place which he has given to God.' The horse was found dead the next morning, and when the chieftain sent two men to kill Patrick, he himself was struck down.

Patrick, according to Muirchu, blessed some water which brought the chieftain and his horse back to life.

Daire then gave Patrick his first choice – the top of the hill, then called *Druimsailech*, 'the ridge of sallows'. The rath upon which the Cathedral stands is still clearly discernible, and although this is probably the Rath of Daire, it may possibly be a later fortification constructed by the builders of the three early churches. The first two little churches which were founded by St Patrick himself were almost certainly made of wattle and daub, and the third church, constructed in stone and known as the *Damhliac Mor,* 'Great Stone Church' was demolished when Primate O'Scannail built its successor in 1268. This was badly damaged by a series of invading armies and warring Irish Chiefs. Further damage was done in the sixteenth century during the Reformation and the following Plantation of Ulster.

The Reformation not only caused structural damage, but also the theft of important relics of the Cathedral. Probably the most important of these was the crosier of St Patrick. According to the legends this crosier was given to St Patrick by a hermit to whom it was delivered by Jesus, hence the name *Bachal Isa* (Staff of Jesus). This crosier was taken to Dublin, stripped of its gems and ornaments, and, with other relics, publicly burnt in 1538, in the High Street. Another relic stolen from the Cathedral, the Black Bell of St Patrick, is now in the National Museum of Ireland.

The Cathedral was completely restored by Lord Beresford in 1834. The work was carried out under the advice of the architect, Lewis Nockalls, who restored St Alban's Abbey; and like St Alban's Armagh, was very much over-restored. The external walls were refaced with freestone and the inside walls were covered with plaster. Windows and doors were ruthlessly altered to conform to the Early English style of architecture, and there is hardly anything today to tell the casual observer that here is Ireland's oldest Cathedral, except one little point. If you stand at the west end of the Cathedral and look up the nave towards the chancel, you will notice that the chancel is out of line and inclined to the north. This is a feature which you may find only in the oldest Irish churches. This slant is generally accepted as a representation of the inclination of Jesus' head on the cross.

William Makepeace Thackeray visited the Cathedral in the early 1840s:

The church is small, but extremely neat, fresh and handsome, almost too handsome; covered with spick-and-span gilding and carved-work in the style of the thirteenth century; every pew as smart and well-cushioned as my lord's own seat in the country church; and for the clergy and their chief, stalls and thrones quite curious for their ornament and splendour. The Primate with his blue ribbon and badge (to whom the two clergymen bow reverently as, passing between them, he enters at the gate of the altar rail) looks like a noble Prince of the Church; and I had heard enough of his magnificent charity and kindness to look with reverence at his lofty handsome features.

What impressed him most, however, was the length of the service:

Will it be believed that the sermon lasted only for 20 minutes? Can this be Ireland? I think this wonderful circumstance impressed me more than any other with the difference between North and South, and, having the Primate's own countenance for the opinion, may confess a great admiration for orthodoxy in this particular.

The oldest part of the present Cathedral is the crypt, where the semi-circular arches date from the ninth century. The crypt contains the vaults of the Caulfield family, Primate Robinson, Baron Rokeby, Primate Lord John George Beresford, Primate Marcus Gervais Beresford, and of many other distinguished people.

In the south transept of St Patrick's Cathedral, Armagh, is the Regimental Chapel of the Royal Irish Fusiliers. On the east wall of the chapel hangs many of the regimental colours presented to the fusiliers during their long and distinguished history, including three sets of colours presented personally by Queen Victoria. Also prominently displayed is the *Book of Remembrance* which contains the names of more than 4,000 men of all ranks, who died on active service during the Boer War, and the First and Second World Wars.

Inside the Cathedral in the north aisle are the remains of an eleventh-century high cross with scenes of the Old and New Testament. This High Cross stood once on the Market Street, but was destroyed in 1813. After laying in the churchyard for over a century, it was more or less reconstructed and placed inside the Cathedral. There is also a collection of pagan stones in the north transept (chapterhouse), which include a figure known as Sheela-na-Gigs which depicts an ancient Irish Chieftain with ears like a horse. Legend has it that every barber who came to cut this Chieftain's hair was put to death, so that the secret of his horse's ears might not be revealed.

Also of enormous interest is the Tandragee Idol, given the name because it stood for some time in the grounds of Ballymore Rectory, Tandragee. It is a half-length figure with close-fitting head-dress or helmet, which covers the upper part of the head, concealing the eyebrows of the protruding eyes. The idol is said to represent one of Ireland's greatest Kings, Nuadha, who was deposed from his throne after losing his arm in battle. His successor, Bres, turned out to be more cruel and oppressive than Nuadha. Complete with an arm he had made for himself out of silver, he seized back his throne. The two-foot tall statuette is said to be a representation of Nuadha holding his silver arm.

In the churchyard north from the Cathedral you can find the burial site of Brian Boru, who died in the Battle of Clontarf in 1014. Brian Boru was too old to participate in the battle and was killed in his tent by a fleeing Viking. A granite commemoration slab in the west wall of the northern transept can be confusing because it only mentions the real name of Brian Boru: Brian Boroimhe. The battle of Clontarf was a bloody affair, with the Norse armies of Dublin and Leinster, being reinforced by troops from Man, and the western and northern isles. Brian Boru, on the other hand, could only muster the support of the south Connaught armies of Uí Maine and Uí Fiachrach Aidne. Nevertheless, they won the day. According to ancient accounts, after the battle the body of Brian, 'high-king of the Irish of Ireland and of the foreigners [the Hiberno-Norse] and of the Britons', along with that of his son Murchad, were brought ceremoniously to Armagh by its abbot and clergy, and there waked for twelve nights, before being buried in a new tomb.

Grouped round the old Cathedral are many noble buildings, including the **Library** which Primate Robinson endowed in 1781, and which ranks amongst the first three in Ireland. Over its porch an inscription in Greek characters is typical of the spirit of the place – '*Pseuches Iatreion*' the 'Medicine Shop of the Soul.' Built to the design of Thomas Cooley, it is constructed of ashlar limestone, and was described by the Ulster Architectural Heritage Society as, 'One of the most perfect architectural set pieces in the City'. The nucleus of the collection is Archbishop Robinson's own library which contains seventeenth- and eighteenth-century books on theology, philosophy, classic and modern literature, voyages and travels, history, medicine, and law. There are also many rare and valuable books such as John Gerson's, *De Praeceptis Decalogi,* printed in Strasbourg in 1488, and Sir Walter Raleigh's, *History of the World*, which was published in 1614. Arguably the most interesting is a copy of Jonathan Swift's, *Gulliver's Travels*, with amendments and markings in Swift's own handwriting.

In 2001, the library received museum status in recognition of its role in the safe-keeping of a wider range of collections, such as Robinson's large collection of engravings known as the 'Rokeby Collection', with examples from the work of Piranesi, Hogarth, and Bartolozzi. It also houses many Irish artefacts collected by Archbishop Marcus Gervais Beresford during his lifetime. There are other items on view including, the Silver Maces presented to Armagh when it became a city for the first time in 1656, and the only foreign flag ever captured on the island of Ireland.

Nearby on Abbey Street is the old **Armagh Infirmary** building, which has

Left: St Patrick's Catholic Cathedral, Armagh.

Below left: Druminargal House.

Below: Tandragee Idol.

been restored and is now the Armagh campus of Queen's University, Belfast. Designed by architect George Ensor, it has something of the feel of a country house stranded in the town. The fourteen-bed hospital was completed in 1774, with eight beds for men and four for women, and the other two for emergencies. By 1888, Bassett states there were seventy-two beds, thirty-six for male and thirty-six for female free patients. There were also two beds for paying patients in a separate ward. There are some interesting memorial plaques in the entrance and the fine original staircase is intact.

The small city centre surrounds Market Square and the main streets are called English Street, Irish Street, and Scotch Street. These three streets roughly mark out the 'Trians', a term for the ancient divisions of the city. To get a better idea of the history and development of the city, a visit to the **St Patrick's Trian Visitor Complex** is a must. Located in the heart of Armagh City on English Street, it incorporates three exhibitions: the Armagh Story traces the story of Armagh's historic pagan monuments through to the arrival of Christianity with St Patrick, Patrick's Testament takes a closer look at the saint's life through his writings, and The Land of Lilliput follows the story of Swift's *Gulliver's Travels*.

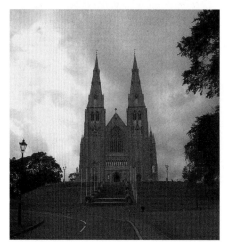

Above left Armagh Public Library.

Above right: Armagh Public Library interior.

Left: Catholic Cathedral, Armagh.

Soon after the Catholic Emancipation Act of 1829, the Roman Catholic archbishops returned to live in Armagh, especially in the person of Archbishop William Crolly. According to James Stuart, in his *Historical Memories of the City of Armagh*, published in 1819:

> Before Emancipation, the primates did not dare to officiate in the town of Armagh, but used to administer the Sacrament of Confirmation in a house, situated just three miles outside, where they likewise held the conferences of the clergy. They also confirmed in the old castle or Fort of Charlemont. Tradition has it that they were not allowed to officiate within the three mile limit.

Across the valley on the opposite hill the twin spires of the National Cathedral of St Patrick are lifted high to heaven, erected by the Roman Catholic Church by National subscription, '*cum Gloire De agus Onorana h'Eireann*', 'To the Glory of God and the Honour of Ireland', and as a memorial to the National Apostle. St Patrick's Cathedral, also known as **Catholic Cathedral** is built opposite the St Patrick's Church of Ireland Cathedral, on Tealach na Licci, of Sandy Hill. There is a legend recorded in the Book of Armagh, which can be interpreted as a vision of St Patrick, that one day a church would be built on Sandy Hill. 'I wonder how many thousands of day labourers gave their mite to its building in the thirty years since the work began', wrote Stephen Gwynn.

Archbishop Crolly laid the foundation stone of the cathedral on St Patrick's Day in 1840. However, work was delayed and disrupted on a number of occasions, notably during the Great Famine (1845-50). In the years following the Great Famine, the funds for the construction was raised by donations from emigrants and a bazaar. Using a bazaar for fundraising was a new phenomena in the 1860s and prominent people donated unique artefacts. The Pope sent an ivory carving of Raphael's, *Madonna Di Foligno*, the Emperor of Austria a specially designed table of inlaid work, and Napoleon II contributed two magnificent vases from the Tuileries. One item, a clock, is still waiting in the Cathedral for its new owner who bought it but forgot to collect. The Cathedral was dedicated for worship in 1873, but the magnificent interior decoration was not completed until the early twentieth century. It was finally consecrated in 1904.

The Cathedral is reached by a seven-terraced flight of broad steps which lead to a spacious platform in front of the western doors. Inside, the visitor finds that the Cathedral is cruciform in plan, comprising nave, aisles, and transepts, with chancel and choir, all of which glistens with mosaics, in a magnificent range of colours. The interior is lofty and of uniform height throughout. At each angle of the western front, is a tower with a slender spire rising to a height of 210 feet and surmounted by a ten-foot cross. In the bell tower is a carillion of thirty-nine bells, the largest weighing 2½ tons. In the south transept is the Sacred Heart altar, containing some of the most precious marbles in the Cathedral while the pulpit is beautifully sculptured and inlaid with various marbles. The high altar is of Carrara marble, and its frontal displays a representation of Leonardo da Vinci's *Last Supper*. The south aisle, approached from the south transept, forms St Brigid's Chapel, and is covered with mosaics illustrating her life while the Lady Chapel, occupying the central part of the chancel, also contains some beautiful mosaics. The north chancel aisle forms St Joseph's Chapel, and on the walls of the great north transept are medallions of Irish saints, and a great five-light window.

The Mall, an elegant tree-lined promenade, is a good place to begin looking around Armagh, and strongly sets the tone of the place. With an attractive park surrounded by some of the city's finest Georgian architecture it is a tranquil spot at the heart of the city. On Rocque's map of 1760, it is named, 'The Common' and 'the Horse Course'. The starting point was near Barrack Street and the fishing post at the bottom of Jenny's Row. Many of the Georgian townhouses along its length had large, balconied, first-floor reception rooms which would have given a good view of the starting and finishing courses. The race course was removed by Primate Robinson for the purpose of utilizing them as a public walk for the inhabitants of the city. In 1803, Coote writes that, 'a very fine wall, or terrace, has been lately enclosed with a dwarf wall, dyke and iron gates, within which is a neat gravel walk, encompassing a lawn, for the enclosing of which Lord Rokeby procured an act of parliament, and is but lately finished'. G.H. Bassett writing in 1888, says that the transformation into a public walk, 'was accomplished by subscription, in a creditable manner. The trees then planted, and some added by a citizen, are now of majestic proportions. Football and cricket matches are played on the green, and the country in the town feature is furnished by the presence of grazing cattle'.

Above: Armagh Gaol.

Above right: Armagh Courthouse.

Right: Fusiliers Museum Sovereign House.

The Mall is appropriately encircled by a number of Armagh's best classical buildings that include the Court House, Sovereign House, the Armagh Museum, and the County Gaol. Erected between 1806 and 1809, the Court House was constructed from a locally quarried limestone known as Armagh Marble. It is designed in the Georgian Classical style with one of the finest front elevations ever created by its architect, Francis Johnston. The Court House has been renovated several times in its history, most recently between 1993 and 1997 after a bomb almost destroyed the building. The original building had two courtrooms and two grand jury rooms, a clerk's office, and the main hallway. Those two courtrooms remain today, but one of the grand jury rooms has been converted into a third courtroom, whilst the other is now a barrister's room. Offices and consultation rooms have been added in a new block at the rear of the old building. The inside of the building has been carefully refurbished, with many original features and plasterwork either restored or reproduced.

Sited exactly opposite the courthouse is the gaol which was built on the site of the old barracks. The main block of the gaol was built in two stages. Firstly, in 1780 the southmost entrance bay with four bays on each side (male prisoners on one side, female on the other) was built. Then in 1819, a second pedimented entrance bay (governor's house), together with a third four-bay block, both identical to the original, were added to the north end. This was organised into three separate prisons: on the left, women, in the centre debtors and on the right, felons. G.H. Bassett visited the gaol in 1888, and commented that:

> the cells in both wards are maintained in perfect condition, the most sensitive nose failing to perceive the faintest trace of that order expected to be found associated with bolts and bars. There are two tiers of cells, one at each side of the ward. An iron gallery surrounds the upper tier, and a substantial rope netting covers the open space, as a precaution against suicide. There are good bathing facilities and the sanitary arrangements throughout are excellent. A well-filled bookcase in the central hall supplies material for improving the mind. During the first month of confinement the prisoner has an opportunity to become acquainted with the 'plank bed' – a bare board. If he takes to it philosophically, he can earn two good conduct marks a day and rise triumphant from the 'plank' to a mattress in thirty days. The cells are each twelve feet by seven, and nine feet high and are heated by hot-air flues. The buildings and premises include three and a half acres. Prisoners are received from the whole of Armagh, Cavan and Monaghan, and from a portion of Down and a portion of Fermanagh.

Executions were common at the gaol, indeed the gallows stood outside the front of the building until 1866, when executions took place behind the impressive prison walls. The last man to be executed at Armagh gaol was Joseph Fee in 1904. In 1920, the entire building became a women's prison which was closed in 1986. It is now in a sad state of neglect. In his book, *Time In Armagh*, poet John Montague sums up the atmosphere of the Mall and its prison:

> And then Armagh, its calm Georgian Mall.
> A student's memory of bells, the carillion
> Echoing from the new Cathedral, glooms
> Over the old walls and sleeping canon,
> The incongruously handsome Women's Prison.

The Regimental Museum of the Royal Irish Fusiliers is situated in 'Sovereign's House, a fine Georgian building dating from 1809. It celebrates the history of the Royal Irish Fusiliers, which is closely associated with the city of Armagh. The museum has interpretative displays covering the history of the Regiment, and the Armagh, Cavan, and Monaghan Militias from 1793 to 1968. There are fine displays of uniforms, trophies, badges, and medals. They are proud owners of the VCs won by Robert Morrow and Geoffrey Cather. The archive includes contemporary letters and diaries, battalion war diaries, and discharge papers. Also of interest are photograph albums, war diaries, and regimental histories. It also has the distinction of being the first house built on the Mall and local tradition states that materials used were surplus to the court house contract. This may well be the case becasue the house was built for Arthur Irwin Kelly, the contractor for the court house. John Claudius Beresford, uncle of the Primate Lord John George Beresford, made a public comment on the coincidence of Mr Kelly's good fortune after which the Court House and Mr Kelly's house were known as, 'The Cat and Kitten'. Kelly was created a Burgess in 1805, and at the end of the same year was appointed Sovereign, a position he held almost continuously until 1837.

Armagh County Museum's unique architecture makes it one of the most distinctive buildings in the city. Ireland's oldest county museum, its extensive collections are based on specimens gathered by the Armagh Natural History and Philosophical Society during the nineteenth century. The exhibitions reveal the rich and varied history of the county, with military costumes, wedding dresses, ceramics, natural history specimens, railway memorabilia, and household items from a bygone age. An impressive art collection includes works by many well-known Irish artists, including the Lurgan-born mystic poet George Russell.

To the north of the Mall, on College Hill, are the Observatory and Royal School. **The Observatory** was founded in the year 1790 by Primate Robinson, on

Left: Armagh Museum.

Below: Armagh Planetarium.

Bottom left: Armagh Observatory.

Bottom right: Armagh Royal School.

Knockamel (The Hill of Honey). It was from here that the *Armagh Star Catalogue* was issued in 1859 – it is still a standard reference amongst astronomers. Presently, around twenty-five astronomers are actively studying stellar astrophysics from the observatory. The Observatory had at one time the largest telescope in Ireland, which can be seen in its original purpose-built dome and some unique clocks and instruments. The Director welcomes visitors if he receives notice of their coming. Next-door to the observatory is the **Planetarium**, which is linked by a short woodland path round the back. The planetarium was built in 1968, and has recently gone through a major refurbishment. It now houses Ireland's first, full dome three-dimensional Digital Theatre. The new projection system accurately recreates the beauty of the night sky, and will take the visitor on a voyage to distant worlds.

Close by is the **Royal School**, which was one of a number of 'free schools'

Above left: Armagh market square *c* 1990.

Above right: Armagh market place in 1810.

created by James I in 1608, to provide an education to the sons of local merchants and farmers during the plantation of Ulster. A boys' school from its inception, the Royal School was amalgamated with Armagh Girls' High School in 1986 to become co-educational. Famous pupils include Lord Castlereagh, Foreign Secretary, and Sir Isaac Corry, Lord Chancellor of the Irish Parliament.

Originally intended to be sited at Mountnorris in South Armagh, the turbulent situation in Ulster at the time led to a move to the relative safety of Armagh City. Despite this precaution, John Starkey, an early headmaster of the school, and his family, were drowned by insurgents during the 1641 Rebellion. The school arrived at its current 27-acre site on College Hill in the 1770s. Arthur Young visited the school just after it had moved to the new site:

> The school is a building of considerable extent, and admirably adapted for the purpose: a more convenient or a better contrived one is nowhere to be seen. There are apartments for a master, a school-room fifty-six feet by twenty-eight, a large dinning room, and spacious, airy dormitories, with every other necessary, and a spacious playground walled in; the whole forming a handsome front: and attention being paid to the residence of the mater (the salary is four hundred pounds a year), the school flourishes, and must prove one of the greatest advantages to the country of anything that could have been established.

In 1823, a number of pupils staged the 'Barring Out', arming and barricading themselves into a dormitory. Their actions were in protest at the cancellation of their usual Wednesday half-day holiday by Dr Guillemard, the headmaster. Dr Guillemard's action was a result of the pupils' failure to identify those responsible for placing an explosive device near the fire in the boarders' common room. The doctor was in the habit of warming himself by this fire in the evening, and was blown across the room by the resulting explosion. The boys brought in bread, cheese, wine, whiskey, beer, and pistols, before barricading themselves in. When the school caretaker attempted to break through, they shot at him. The local militia was called but took no action. After three days the boys surrendered and were soundly flogged by the same caretaker at whom they had shot.

To the south of the city, on the road to Monaghan can be found the **The**

Armagh Friary.

Armagh Friary.

Primate's Palace, a fine old Georgian Mansion, built by Primate Robinson. It stands in the palace demesne and contains many fine paintings, including portraits of all the Primates since Adam Loftus, who came to the Archiepiscopal Chair in 1562, besides a number of royal portraits. The palace was commissioned in 1770 by Archbishop Robinson as his new primate's palace. The architect for the imposing building was Thomas Cooley, with later additions in 1825, by Francis Johnston. The building was too large and in much need of restoration when the Church decided to sell it to the local Council in the mid-1970s. The council set about restoring the building to its former glory but at the same time, making it a working building. It now houses the District Council offices. The public are now able to make use of the beautiful grounds, which were part of the palace boundary, and can tour the other buildings situated in the demesne.

A side door from the Primate's palace gives access to the archbishop's private chapel. Built in 1781 for Archbishop Robinson, it was, like the Palace, designed by Thomas Cooley, and finished after his death by Francis Johnston. The chapel takes the form of a classical garden temple, faced on all elevations with ashlar limestone and was originally constructed for the Primate, clergy, and staff. The Archbishop's throne is placed in the middle of one of the long walls, and there is a fireplace on the opposite wall. The windows are in memory of John George Beresford, Archbishop of Armagh 1822-1862. Now deconsecrated, the chapel is used for concerts and can be visited as part of a guided tour.

In the palace demesne there are the ruins of an old Franciscan friary, founded in 1266, by Primate O'Scanlan, of which now only the western archway and some fragments of high walls remain. The friary was amongst those suppressed by Henry VIII in 1542, and in 1561 it was burned by Shane O'Neill, who at the same time destroyed the Cathedral and the houses of the city, in order to prevent their occupation by Crown Forces. In 1596, the ground was the scene of a struggle between the troops of Hugh O'Neill and General Norris. The interior was used as a burying ground until about 1740. Gormlaith, wife of Domhnall O'Neill, King of Ulster, was buried in the Friary precincts on the 14 April 1353.

The Franciscan friary had long been a picturesque ruin by the time George Henry Bassett visited Armagh in the late 1880s:

Time has dealt severely with the walls, but the ravages are to a great extent hidden by ivy. Several of the broken arches are wrapped in mantles of ivy springing from leaders of tree-like proportions. One of the number, still flourishing, appears to be larger than the famous ivy in Muckross abbey, Killarney, said to be over 200 years old.

Bassett found that, during the eighteenth century, parts of the friary had been demolished. 'Out-offices, which stood close to the ruin, in the last century, were removed by Lord John George Beresford. About twelve years ago the walls fell.' Other monuments had succumbed to the ravages of time. 'The Christian character of the people of Armagh was attested by the presence of many crosses in the thoroughfares. The last one disapperard in 1813. It stood in Market Square. A portions is preserved in the Cathedral.'

From the friary, a pleasant woodland path known as Lady Anne's Walk leads to **St Brigid's Well**. The path is named after Eleanor Alexander, the gifted daughter of Cecil Frances (author of many hymns including *Once in Royal David's City*)and Primate William Alexander. Her novels include *Lady Anne's Walk; The Rambling Rector* (1904) and *The Lady of the Well*. St Brigid born in the mid-fifth century at Faughart, near Dundalk, is associated with Armagh through her friendship with St

Patrick. According to the *Book of Armagh* 'Between St. Patrick and St. Brigid, the columns of the Irish, there was so great a friendship of charity that they had but one heart and one mind. Through him and through her Christ performed many miracles.' St Brigid's Well, was once a place which drew considerable pilgrimages; the waters were generally used for eye troubles, though they were considered good for all ills. The well was formerly overhung by 'gentry' bushes, on which rags of all colours could be seen fluttering in the breeze. It is said that Lady Anne brought some of the waters of the well to Queen Victoria when her brother, the Primate, went to pay his respects to the Queen on her accession.

The Palace Stables Heritage Centre is a wonderfully-restored eighteenth-century stable block, formerly part of the estate belonging to the Archbishop of Armagh right up until the 1970s. This fabulous visitor centre takes the visitor back to the hustle and bustle of the late eighteenth century. The guided tour takes in some of the estate's most historic buildings including the Georgian Kitchen, the kitchen walled garden, the Primate's Chapel and the Archbishop's Palace.

Chapter 7

West from Armagh

If Armagh is Ireland's Canterbury, then **Navan Fort**, or Emain Macha, is Ulster's Camelot. Just three miles west of Armagh on the A28, it is the location for the oldest group of Irish heroic tales, featuring the warriors of the Red Branch as recounted in the medieval chronicle known as the *Annals of Ulster*. The Annals gives us a picture of what Armagh was like before the arrival of Christianity set as it is in the first century BC. It was a time of magic, ancient gods, heroes, and endless warfare. Such was the prestige of the site that Emain Macha was included on a second-century gazetteer of Ireland compiled by the Greek geographer, Ptolemy. Two important places are located in Ulster, *Regia* or 'royal palace' and, *Isamnion*, the latter sounding linguistically similar to *Eamhain*.

There are two famous tales about the foundation of *Emain Macha*. In the first tale a warrior queen named Macha ruled over all of Ireland and married one of her rivals, Cimbaeth. She then took on her other enemies by luring them into the woods one by one and defeating each of them. According to the *Annals of the Four Masters*, Macha then, 'placed them in great servitude, until they should erect the fort of Emain, that it might always be the chief city of the Ulstermen'. She did this by marking off a circuit of Navan Fort with a brooch and the early Irish believed that the name Emain came from the old Irish word for a neck-brooch, 'eo-mhuin'.

The other story is that a mysterious Fairy Lady named Macha came to live with a widower and gave him great luck in life. Unfortunately, he went to a fair one day and boasted to the king of Ulster that his wife could outrun the king's horses. The woman was taken and ordered to race the king's chariot or see her husband beheaded. At the time she was pregnant and, although she pleaded to have the race postponed, she was forced to run. She won the race and at the finish gave birth to twins, a boy and a girl. Before she died she cursed the Ulstermen for the

Above and opposite: Navan Fort.

next nine generations for making her race and Ulster's warriors were afflicted with a debilitating disease for nine days whenever there was a great crisis. In this story, the name of *Emain Macha* was believed to mean 'twins of Macha.'

By the first century BC, Ulster was ruled by a great king called Conchobar MacNessa who had his capital at *Emain Macha*, but it is his nephew and foster son Cúchulainn who is remembered as the great hero of early Irish literature. Originally named Setanta, he was the child of the Danaan god, Lugh, and Deichtine, sister of Conchobar MacNessa. He earned the name Cúchulainn at the age of seven when he followed the royal household to the home of the wealthy smith, Culann, where a great feast was being held in honour of the king. Setanta arrived late, only to be attacked by the fierce hound which Culann had left to guard the entrance to his home. Setanta killed the hound by dashing it against a rock or, in some versions of the story, by striking the hound with a sliotar. The royal household were amazed but Culann was distraught at the loss of his hound. Setanta promised to take the hound's place until a new one could be raised, earning him the nickname Cúchulainn, 'hound of Culann'.

As he grew to manhood, Cúchulainn proved himself to be Ulster's greatest warrior. The Druids in the Hall of Heroes warn him that his life would be short but he defiantly declares, 'I care not whether I die tomorrow or next year, if only my deeds live after me.' Cúchulainn's greatest deed is recounted in the *Táin Bó Cúailnge* or *The Cattle Raid of Cooley* when he single-handedly defends Ulster from the army of Connaught. The Connaught army was led by Queen Medb whose objective was to steal the stud bull, Donn Cúailnge. The men of Ulster were disabled by Macha's curse, so Cúchulainn prevented Medb's army from advancing further by invoking the right of single combat at fords. He defeats champion after champion in a stand-off lasting months. During the battle he is driven into a terrifying battle frenzy or *ríastrad*, described in detail by the chronicles:

The first warp-spasm seized Cúchulainn, and made him into a monstrous thing, hideous and shapeless, unheard of. His shanks and his joints, every knuckle and angle and organ from head to foot, shook like a tree in the flood or a reed in the stream. His body made a furious twist inside his skin, so that his feet and shins switched to the rear and his heels and calves switched to the front ... On his head the temple-sinews stretched to the nape of his neck, each mighty, immense, measureless knob as big as the head of a month-old child ... he sucked one eye so deep into his head that a wild crane couldn't probe it onto his cheek out of the depths of his skull; the other eye fell out along his cheek. His mouth weirdly distorted: his cheek peeled back from his jaws until the gullet appeared, his lungs and his liver flapped in his mouth and throat, his lower jaw struck the upper a lion-killing blow, and fiery flakes large as a ram's fleece reached his mouth from his throat ... The hair of his head twisted like the tange of a red thornbush stuck in a gap; if a royal apple tree with all its kingly fruit were shaken above him, scarce an apple would reach the ground but each would be spiked on a bristle of his hair as it stood up on his scalp with rage.

Cúchulainn by John Duncan.

It was only by magic that Cúchulainn was eventually pierced by his own spear. With great difficulty, holding in his entrails, Cúchulainn tied himself to a high stone by a lake, because, 'he did not wish to die either sitting or lying: it was standing that he wished to meet his death'. His faithful horse protected him as he died, and it was only when a raven alighted on his shoulder that his enemies knew he was dead.

Emain Macha was destroyed after being ravaged in internal wars within Ulster some time before the arrival of Christianity. After its abandonment, Emain Macha continued to exert a certain prestige. In the Middle Ages, it was a regular place of assembly and fairs, which were either held within the enclosure itself or the surrounding area. One twelfth-century text also relates that many Ulstermen would not visit *Emain Macha* on Halloween because of a legend that they would be driven mad and die the next day. In 1387, the Ulster king, Niall O'Neill, built a house at *Emain*. He did this for two reasons: he wanted to please the poets and scholars who venerated the memory of the ancient cultural centre of Ulster, and he wanted to associate the O'Neill family, the new rulers of Ulster, with its former capital. The cartographer, Richard Bartlett, who accompanied Lord Deputy Mountjoy on his campaign to crush the rebellion of the Earl of Tyrone towards the end of the sixteenth century, was much impressed with Ulster's ancient capital. In two of his maps, Bartlett indicated the location of Navan Fort and labelled it, 'Owene Maugh, the ancient seat of the Kings of Ulster'.

Archaeological excavations during the 1960s, revealed that Navan had been settled by early farmers as early as 5,000 years ago. Archaeologists found metal objects typical of the native late Bronze-Age culture of Ireland in the earliest houses on the site. These include a bronze axe, bronze spearheads, and a bronze sickle. Generations later, new houses were built, and the objects excavated from this area, including a sword scabbard typical of the Early Iron Age in Britain and the Continent. The high status of the site is also demonstrated by the discovery of the skull of a barbary ape, showing that whoever resided there at the time had connections with North Africa and the Mediterranean area during the Iron Age.

Navan Fort remains the most important archaeological and historical site in Northern Ireland, and a walk around the site allows the visitor to follow the landscape of legendary Ulster. What survives is a large earthwork of circular plan 250m (820 ft) in diameter, surrounded by a bank and ditch. Unusually, the ditch is inside the bank, suggesting it was not built for defensive purposes. The impressive earthwork encloses two monuments on the hilltop, a ring barrow (Iron Age burial site) and a large mound. Excavations in the 1960s revealed that the mound was a composite structure, built in 95 BC at the end of a long sequence of earlier activity. A huge, circular, wooden construction was raised, 40m in diameter, with five rings of oak posts (275 in all) aligned around a large central post. The timber structure was later filled with limestone blocks to form a cairn 3m high and the whole structure was set ablaze. Finally, a deep deposit of clay and sods was placed over the surface of the cairn to form the high mound which visitors see today. From the top of this mound the visitor can enjoy a superb view of the surrounding countryside, a view that includes the pinnacles of Armagh's two Cathedrals.

There is free access to the fort but to appreciate the site's history it is best to go into the **Navan Centre**. It has creatively been built into the side of a grass bank to look like a large Bronze-Age cairn. There are detailed exhibitions displaying finds from the fort and the nearby man-made pond, and an imaginative visual presentation of the legends associated with the site, including the story of Cúchulainn. There is also an exhibition about the evacuation of the fort between 1961 and 1971, with old photographs and an enigmatic hologram showing how the fort's appearance has changed from the Bronze Age to the present day.

A short distance to the north-west of Navan Fort is **Haughey's Fort**, a hill fort named after the farmer who owned the land in the later nineteenth century. The large hilltop enclosure consists of an oval enclosure, 350m across at its widest point, surrounded by two concentric ditches. Inside the enclosure another ditch encloses an area 150m in diameter. Archaeological excavation shows that it was occupied in the late Bronze Age from 1100 to 900 BC, after which it was abandoned. Some artefacts discovered were of Iron-Age date, however, suggesting that it was later reoccupied. It was contemporary with the nearby artificial pool, known as the **King's Stables**. This is a pool about 25m across and about 4m deep. A small test excavation in the pool found animal bones, moulds for swords, and part of the skull of a young man. The findings suggest that this was a ritual pool used to deposit offerings to gods.

There are probably many more sites in the vicinity of Navan, since a number of bronze artefacts have been found in the neighbouring fields. Mr and Mrs Hall wrote in the early 1840s:

> Various relics of antiquity are dug up from time to time in its vicinity; indeed, so numerously are they found that a cottager seldom occupies a day in delving a field without striking his spade against some record of long ages part – arrow-heads continually, sometimes a spear-head or skene, and now and then a brooch or ring of costly workmanship.

A few miles outside Armagh along the A3 the small village of **Milford** takes the visitor back to the textile industry of the nineteenth century. Until recent years the village consisted of three streets of terraced houses, but in modern times several new housing estates have been built. The village grew up around the linen mill owned by the McCrum family in the nineteenth century. According to Bassett who visited Milford during its industrial heyday:

> The inhabitants, with few exceptions, work in the weaving factory of Messrs Robert McCrum & Co. Mr. William McCrum, some years deceased, built a mill here in 1808, and it is claimed to have been the first in Ulster used for spinning flax by the dry process. All the machinery for it was brought from Leeds. In 1850 Mr. Robert G. McCrum, J.P., changed the spinning mill into a factory for the weaving of damasks. At present there are 270 looms in full operation, driven by a 200 horse-power steam engine, and a turbine of 120 horse. About 450 people are constantly employed. Diapers and towellings are also woven at Milford, and yarn bleaching is done for the use of the concern only. Since 1850 Mr. Robert G. McCrum has made substantial structural additions to the factory, and has almost entirely built the village, of which it may be truly said, that it is a model of cleanliness and good order, the humblest dwelling bearing evidence internally and externally of a beneficent proprietary control. Mr. McCrum's handsome private residence, Milford House, stands in a richly-planted and highly ornamented park at the verge of the village, and commands a beautiful view of the surrounding country.

Nearby is Milford House, built by Robert McCrum who devised the most technologically advanced house in Ireland, the first in Ireland to have electricity and with its own indoor waterfall. From 1936 to 1965, it was home to the Manor House School, the only private school of its kind in Northern Ireland. Today the building is in a sad state of disrepair and is registered on the Buildings at Risk Northern Ireland catalogue. The Gate Lodge on the other hand has been restored and is open to the public. It houses a museum of family costumes, furniture and silver returned to Milford after an absence of over seventy years.

It was the family home of William McCrum remembered today as the inventor of the penalty kick. A former Irish League goalkeeper, it was as a member of the Irish Football Association in June 1890, that he proposed the idea of the penalty kick in order to stop the prevalent practice at the time of defenders professionally fouling an attacking player in order to stop a goal. The idea offended many who valued the Victorian idea of the amateur gentleman sportsman and refused to accept the idea that any gentleman could act in an unsporting manner. It was finally approved as number 13 in the Laws of the Game in June 1891. The 'William McCrum Memorial Park' in the village is dominated by a bust of William McCrum sculpted by Belfast artist, David Pettigrew in 2005.

Above: Milford.

Milford *c. 1900.*

Tynan Abbey *c. 1900.*

Eight miles west from Armagh, and one mile from the Monaghan border, **Tynan** is a village in the heart of delightful countryside. Tynan was the site of a church founded by St Uinnic, the name derived from *Tuinean*, 'place of the (man-made) watercourse'. This name can be taken as evidence that a mill was an important feature of the foundation. According to Sir Charles Coote writing in 1804:

> The town, which is situated on an eminence, is inconsiderable as to the number or neatness of its houses, but it has an excellent church with handsome steeple; without the churchyard is a relick of antiquity, an oblong stone of about eighteen inches square and four feet long, set up on a large block stone, and capped with another, which is square, having faces concaved, and this crowned with a smaller one.

The eighth-century cross he refers to is still the most important feature of the village. It is thirteen feet, five inches high, but until 1844 it had lain broken and neglected. Portions of it have been restored, but the lowest part of the shaft is ancient and bears a much-defaced sculptured representation of Adam and Eve being tempted by the Serpent.

Three other crosses stand in the demesne of **Tynan Abbey** and are perhaps a little later in date than Tynan Cross. The Well Cross was brought from Glenarb by Sir James Stronge and placed on an arch above a well. It stands eight feet high and is the most striking of the three demesne crosses. It is of the solid disc or unpierced type. The Island Cross, so-called because it was placed on an island in the demesne, is also eight feet high. It is much weathered, has a restored lower shaft, and was brought, like the Well Cross, from Glenarb. The Terrace Cross stands near the house at the end of a fine avenue of yew trees. This is a very handsome cross, which stands at eleven feet, and it is ornamented with interlacing and curved designs in lozenge and circular patterns.

The original house on this site, built before 1703, was called Fairview and belonged to the Manson family. It was acquired by the Stronges through the marriage of Dr John Stronge and Elinor Manson. At this time Fairview was described by Thomas Ashe as, a 'very pretty house, well timbered and regularly built. It is two stories high. There are good chambers and garrets above staires, a handsome parlour, a common Hall, a Kitchen Sellars and their Convenient Offices a Good Stable Barne and Cow house a Good Garden and Orchard.' It became Tynan Abbey some time between 1810 and 1820, and was enlarged in the Tudor-Gothic style around between 1820 and 1830. Sir Bernard Burke described it in 1855 'as a spacious house in the abbey style, and has a picturesque appearance, bearing a very happy semblance of an ancient edifice, a deception which is not a little heightened by the nature of the surrounding countryside.'

On 21 January 1981, eighty-six-year-old Sir Norman Stronge and his only son, James, forty-eight (both former MPs), were killed by the Provisional IRA. The Stronge family home was then burnt to the ground. Tynan Abbey was demolished in 1998, due to the unstable structure of the ruin. All that remains is the arch of the front door surround. Today there are three gate lodges to the Tynan estates, which are listed buildings. The South Lodge, on Middletown Road, was designed by W.J. Barrie in 1860. Lemnagore was built in 1817 by John Nash, as was the grandiose Castle Lodge, situated on a sharp bend on the Middletown Road.

Tynan Abbey Gate Lodge.

Above: Tynan Cross and church.

Left: Tynan Abbey *c.* 1920s.

Just to the south-east of Tynan is the very fine treble-ringed fort of **Lislooney**, the Fort of the First Day of August. A little south of Tynan is **Middletown**, the frontier post for crossing the border into Co. Monaghan. The old Gaelic name for Middletown was Kilcanavan meaning, 'Canavan's wood' or 'Canavan's church'. It was subsequently named Middletown by the Hamilton family because of its central position between Armagh, Monaghan, Keady, Celedon, and Glaslough. Its early development was associated with Dr Stern, the former bishop of Clougher, who owned seven townlands in the area, including Middletown. After his death in 1745, income from these townlands was dispensed to many charitable causes and developments in the village. According to Lewis in 1837:

This places owes its present prosperity to Dr. Sterne, a former bishop of Clogher who in the latter part of the last century bequeathed the then village of Middletown, eight townlands in this parish, and five in the adjoining parish of Donagh, in the county of Monaghan, to trustees (incorporated by an act of the Irish parliament passed in 1772), who have expended considerable sums for the benefit of the tenantry in general, and in the erection of a market-house, school-house, dispensary, and fever hospital at Middletown. The town consists of two streets crossing each other at right angles; and contained, in 1831, 160 houses, which number has been since increased to 187; several of the houses are large and well built. An extensive distillery, with machinery on an improved principle, was established here in 1831, by Mr Matthew Johnston: it produces annually about 80,000 gallons of whiskey, and consumes on an average 1500 barrels of malt, and 12,000 barrels of raw grain. The distillery has caused the establishment of markets for grain on Wednesday and Saturday, and there is a market on Thursday for provisions. Fairs are held on the first Thursday in each month for horses, cattle and pigs. Here is a station of the constabulary police, and petty sessions are held on alternate Wednesdays.

The convent of St Louis was founded in 1875. Of particular note is a beautiful marble altar situated, inside which was erected by James Pearse, father of Willie and Padraig who played a prominent role in the 1916 Easter Rising in Dublin. St John's Catholic church was built in around 1826, and has a protruding square bell tower on the northern side. The Market House, built by the Sterne Trustees in 1829, has been newly refurbished and continues to be used as an important community facility. During the Troubles, the village was dominated by a large British Army checkpoint, but that has been removed.

World heavyweight-boxing champion, Joe Coburn, was born in Middletown, in 1835. In 1862, he claimed the championship from John Carmel Heenan thanks to Heenan's refusal to fight him. Coburn held the title until 1866, when he retired. According to the *Brooklyn Daily Eagle* for 12 June 1863:

Coburn is a man who stands full five feet nine inches in height. He is finely proportioned, and physically speaking he is a handsome looking man. His shoulders and chest are broad and deep, his limbs long and well rounded, his head is rather small and round, with his chair closely cropped ... His superiority in the ring is due mainly to his quickness of movement, rather than great physical strength. He delivers a blow like a pistol shot, and jumps back in an instant, and is on his guard before his opponent can return the compliment, inflicting punishment without receiving any in return.

About a mile from Middletown, and almost on the Border, is the ruin of **Ardgonnell Castle**, with the west wall, and portions of the north and south walls still standing. In the west wall are two fine fireplaces with elaborate stone surrounds. Before 1608, this castle belonged to Sir Henry Oge O'Neill, and in 1631, to Sir Turlough O'Neill, but it was forfeited in the wars of 1641 and much damaged. It was rebuilt by Sir Robert Hamilton in about 1668 and became known as Mount Hamilton, but locally it is still called Ardgonnell.

South of Middletown, at **Rathtrillick**, the Fort of the Three Pillar Stones, is a splendid triple-ringed earthern fort, in which, in the year 1848, was found a fine bronze axe-head now to be seen in the Armagh County Museum. In the meadows at the base of the hill there is a raised earthen ring without any trench. This is locally known as 'The Ould Forth', and is associated with the fairies.

Left: Tynan Cross.

Below: Joe Coburn.

Killylea, a few miles to the north-east of Tynan, is a small picturesque village slightly to the west of Armagh City, in the northern part of the county. The village originally formed part of an endowment of land to Trinity College Dublin. In 1610, the Revd Robert Maxwell arrived from Scotland to become Dean of Armagh, and for 300 years his family was associated with the area. Set on a hill, St Mark's church was built in 1832. A clock tower and a chancel were new additions in 1854 and 1874 respectively. Another building of note is Fellow's Hall which was originally built in 1762, for the Maxwell family. Built in local Armagh limestone, it includes Italian influences from a later remodelling between 1853 and 1857. The name is derived from the fact that Trinity College Dublin had for centuries been the principal landowners in the region. In the past, Killylea was noted for its monthly fair. According to Coote in 1804:

> The village of Killyleagh consists of but one long street, which is very tedious, as it stands on a very seep hill; the houses are well built of lime and stone, with a clean and neat exterior. This village is not remarkable for any trade, but on the last Friday in each month a fair is held, principally attended by dealers in horses.

Killylea was at the centre of many important historical events during the seventeenth century. The best known is the massacre at the 'Corr Bridge' at Killylea, which took place in May 1642. At the height of the rising against the settler population of Ulster, an army led by Phelim O'Neill rounded up and drowned a large number at Killylea. The total given of those drowned vary a great deal from 38 to 144. Thomas Chambers was staying in Tynan at that time and said that twenty people were taken from that village alone and drowned in the river a mile away.

South of Killylea is **Keady**, a thriving market town which was once a famous linen centre. A place called Sergeant's Town appears on several maps from around 1600, and has been identified from its position as Keady. Keady, in the form given by local Irish speakers, *An Cheideadh*, 'the flat-topped hill', seems not to have existed before the mid-eighteenth century. Legend tells of Cairbre, an early Celtic Chieftain at Rathcarbry near the town, who married a Spanish princess at the royal settlement of *Emain Macha* in 370BC. The first patent to hold fairs there was applied for by Trinity College Dublin in 1758. However, Lewis says that in about 1750, the water power of the area, 'attracted the attention of some enterprising Englishmen' who applied it to the linen trade, in what was up to that time almost an 'uncultivated heath'. The importance of the River Callan is underlined by the Ordnance Survey Map of 1834, where no fewer than twenty beetling mills are marked along the river between Darkley and Tassagh. The landscape around Keady

Killylea church, St Mark's.

Above: Keady Mill.

Right: Kirk Monument Keady.

is still scattered with relics from Ulster's linen heyday, including many mills beside the region's little lakes and rivers. Today the most interesting non-industrial architecture is supplied by the two main churches. St Matthew's church was erected by Archbishop Robinson at his own expense, in 1775, although not consecrated until 1782. A handsome stained-glass chancel window commemorates William Gardiner, of Annvale, who died in 1883. The Roman Catholic church also stands on a hill. It is a large edifice, with a fine pinnacled tower, completed in 1861.

The centre of Keady is dominated by a granite and freestone monument, executed in 1871, to the industrialist and politician, William Kirk, to whom the village owes its early prosperity. Kirk's Annvale establishment employed around 600 hands, and his Darkley works employed upwards of 700 at the end of the nineteenth century. The Kirk monument bears the inscription, 'Erected by many friends in remembrance of William Kirk. For forty years he was the mainspring of the industrial activity and social progress of this town and district'. The manufacture of linen was already well-established in the area, but Kirk harnessed the rich natural resources, and the skills and manpower that were already there from the days when it was no more than a cottage industry. He bought over the Annvale factory in 1837, when it was mainly concerned with the finishing processes, but by the 1840s the complex was weaving as well as bleaching and dyeing.

William Kirk also played a major role in the prosperity of **Darkely**, two miles from Keady. He took over the spinning mill in 1845, and the Darkely works soon expanded to cover 137 acres, boasting 200 power looms manned by 700 persons. The mill was operated by the second largest, if not the largest, water wheel in Europe. To get a better idea of Keady and Darkley's industrial heyday, you should visit the Old Mill in the centre of the town, which has been converted into a modern visitor centre, café, and community enterprise resource. The building is complete with its own millwheel and acts as the entrance to a beautiful riverside walk.

At **Derrynoose**, not far away, is an ancient foundation dating from the beginning of the fourteenth century, and this district is especially rich in souterrains, and ring forts. The remains of Listrakelt church, which was the ancient church of the Parish of Derrynoose, the Island of the Oak Grove, are still traceable in the churchyard, with a plan measuring roughly 70 feet by 26. According to tradition, the north side of the churchyard was reserved for the burial of still-born infants. The Holy Well here, known as St Malachy's Well, was long a place of pilgrimage and the waters were known as a cure for almost all ills.

About two miles north of Keady is the tiny village of **Tassagh**, named after St Tassagh who founded it, and lying in a lovely valley. Here, there is an ancient Culdee burial ground and a unique group of three double-ringed forts. Local tradition also states that there was a monastery here, but there is no recorded early history of the site nor any definite link with St Tassach. Reputed to have lived in the fifth century, St Tassach was a craftsman and is said to have made a receptacle for the Cross of Jesus, one of the treasures of the See of Armagh. The first mound within the cemetery adjacent to the entrance gate is 11 to 12 feet above the level of the road. At the rear of the cemetery, the inner ring of ground remains formidable in parts, while the outer ring falls away into a ten-foot-deep drain which joins the tributary. Also at Tassagh is a substantial beetling-mill, which stands in the shadow of the imposing Tassagh Viaduct. The Tassagh Viaduct was erected in 1905-06 to carry the Castleblayney, Keady, and Armagh Railway across the Callan Valley.

South of Keady is **Carrigatuke Mountain**, which is believed to be the mystical home of King Lir. One of the most beautiful tales in Irish literature, the mythical king remarries after the death of his first wife. His second wife, Aoife, jealous of her four step-children, turns them into swans. After 900 unhappy years of exile they return to their ancestral home on Carrigatuke Mountain, to find it deserted. In despair, they then fly to *Inis Gluaire*, an island off Co Mayo, where they are well-treated by a holy man, who is a disciple of St Patrick. Shortly afterwards, they resume their human form as four very old people, and before they die, they are baptised.

Darkley *c.* 1900.

Today Carrigatuke Mountain is covered with dense coniferous forestry planta-
tions. A well-signposted viewpoint offers a superb perspective of the South Armagh
landscape. From the top, the visitor can enjoy an impressive view of the area as far as
Meath in the south, and even Roscommon to the southwest. It is easy to understand
why this part of Armagh has been described as a miniature Lake District, with lots of
little irregular lakes studded with islands, and placed within countless rolling hills.

Chapter 8

From Armagh to Newry

The A28 takes the visitor south from Armagh to the city of **Newry.** One of the principal routes in the county, and once the mail coach road from Armagh to Dublin, it did not always have an enviable reputation. Sir Charles Coote wrote of it in 1804, 'The turnpike road from Armagh to Newry is perhaps, the worst in Ireland as a public road, and is a disgrace to an opulent county'. Things had improved by the 1830s according to Ordnance Survey which described that portion of it passing through Markethill as 'macadamised and kept in good repair at the expense of the county.'

A few miles to the south of Armagh is the village of **Markethill** founded by a Scottish family, the Achesons of Gosford, or Goseford, Haddingtonshire (East Lothian), who received a grant of 1,000 acres (4km²) from King James I in 1610. The Achesons built a strong castle at Cloncarney in around 1617, but it was destroyed in the war of 1641. It was replaced with a manor house, visited by Jonathan Swift, in the late 1720s. Swift liked to stay in his friend's houses taking with him his own manservant and his dogs. Sir Arthur Acheson, aged forty in 1728, was the deeply respectable, if rather dull, MP for Mullingar and Sheriff of Co. Armagh. His wife Anne was more fun. Swift had known her father, the Hon. Phillip Savage, a former Chancellor of the Exchequer in Ireland. His reason for staying on (plus his two dogs and two horses) he told his friend, playwright R.B Sheridan during his first visit, was that he wanted to be there for, 'planting and pruning time, etc. I hate Dublin, and love the retirement here, and the civility of my hosts'.

Swift paid three visits to Markethill, staying from three to eight months at a time between 1728 and 1730. Swift commented that Co. Armagh, 'excepting it's cursed roads, and want of downs to ride, is the best part I have seen of Ireland.' His verdict on Markethill was that it was, 'situated in the midst of a fertile country,

Markethill.

the extensive demesne and splendid castle of Gosford, the property of Viscount Gosford, adding greatly to its beauty.'

Although there is a drawing of the earlier house by Cornelius Varley in the Armagh County Museum collection entitled, *Gosford Manor, Markethill* and dated 1808, little is known about it. It was approached by an entrance from the old county road, through a double-gate lodge, between the ponds, or basins as they were then called. This feature was retained as part of the nineteenth-century landscaping of the demesne, even though the county road was moved westward to its pre-bypass line. Swift first came to Markethill in June 1728, and stayed until February 1729. He was back in June that year for a three- or four-month sojourn, leaving in September but reappeared in June 1730, and again remained until September. By then he had probably outstayed his welcome for he was a self-centred, rude, and difficult guest, as he unrepentantly recognised in the poem, 'Lady Acheson Weary of the Dean':

The Dean wou'd visit Market-hill,
Our Invitation was but slight
I said – Why – Let him if he will,
And so I bid Sir Arthur write.
His manners would not let him wait,
Least we should think ourselves neglected,
And so we saw him at our Gate
Three Days before he was expected.
After a Week, a Month, a Quarter,
And Day succeeding after Day,
Says not a Word of his Departure
Tho' not a Soul would have him stay.
I've said enough to make him blush
Methinks, or else the Devil's in't,
But he cares not for it a Rush,
Nor for my Life will take a Hint.
But you, my Life, may let him know,
In civil Language, if he stays
How deep and foul the Roads may grow,
And that he may command the Chaise.
Or you may say – my Wife intends,
Tho' I should be exceeding proud,
This Winter to invite some Friends,
And Sir I know you hate a Crowd.
Or, Mr. Dean – I should with Joy
Beg you would here continue still
But we must go to Aghnacloy;
Or Mr. Moor will take it ill.
The House Accounts are daily rising
So much his Stay do's swell the bills;
My dearest Life it is surprizing,
How much he eats, how much he swills.
His Brace of Puppies how they stuff,
And they must have three Meals a Day,
Yet never think they get enough;

His Horses too eat all our Hay.
Oh! if I could, how I would maul
His Tallow Face and Wainscot Paws,
His Beetle-brows and Eyes of Wall,
And make him soon give up the Cause.
Must I be every Moment chid
With skinny, boney, snip and lean,
Oh! that I could but once be rid
Of that insulting Tyrant Dean.

In 1728, he sent a letter from Dublin to Alexander Pope, the poet and a friend from his London days, expressing his satisfaction with his reception at Markethill. He wrote:

I live very easily in the country: Sir Acheson is a man of Sense, and a scholar, has a good voice, and my Lady a better; she is perfectly well bred, and desirous to improve her understanding, which is very good, but cultivated too much like a fine Lady. She was my pupil there, and severely chid when she read wrong; with that, and walking and making twenty little amusing improvements, and writing family verses of mirth by way of libels On my Lady, my time past very well and in great order; infinitely better than here, where I see no creature but my servants and my old Presbyterian house-keeper, denying myself to every body till I shall recover my ears.

Given his rather irascible temperament, the Achesons must have been relieved when Swift decided not to build a house on a site still called Drapier's Hill after one of his most controversial publications, *The Drapier Letters*. The Dean's walk and his chair, a stone seat overlooking the old road, and the Dean's Well also remain as reminders of Swift's time at Markethill.

Swift was a demanding guest as his treatment of Anna Acheson became clear. He made her read Bacon and Milton for hours every day, and veered between raging violently at her ignorance, and being, 'so indulgent, and so mild, As if I were a darling child'.

When he was ill with his recurrent deafness and giddiness at Markethill, he was looked after, and the family were, 'so kind to speak loud enough for me to hear them'. He complained about the cooking, interfered in the wine cellar and the dairy, and gave orders to servants and gardeners without referring to his hosts. Swift had ceased to charm or amuse Sir Arthur, who was introspective, ungregarious, and an indoor man. Too courteous or too depressed to complain about the antics of Swift and his wife, he withdrew into himself. Swift described him in his usual graphic terms:

Dean Swift's Well.

Whoses uncommunicative heart,
Will scarce one precious word impart:
Still rapt in speculations deep,
His outward senses fast asleep;
Who, while I talk, a song will hum,
Or, with his fingers, beat the drum;
Beyond the skies transports his mind,
And leaves a lifeless corpse behind.

Swift continued to see Lady Acheson in Dublin in the early 1730s, telling Charles Ford, 'She is a perfect Dublin rake, sits up late, loses her money, and goes to bed sick.' By that time, she had left her husband and lived with her mother on the north side of Dublin Bay at Baldoyle, where she died in 1737.

Gosford Castle.

During his time at Gosford, Swift devised the existing nature walks throughout the grounds, where he composed poems. The manor house in which he stayed, however, has practically disappeared. In 1819, Archibald Acheson, 2nd Earl of Gosford, commissioned the construction of **Gosford Castle**. The Earl who was the great grandson of Swift's host, employed Thomas Hooper as architect. The castle was not finished until the 1850s. The style of Gosford is that of Norman Revival, it being one of the few examples of this in the world. It was regarded by Robin Fredden, Secretary of the National Trust in 1952, as 'one of the most original buildings of the first half of the nineteenth century'. He further noted that it was 'reputed to be the largest pile in Ireland', having some 150 rooms.

The 4th Earl was forced to sell the castle's contents in 1921, and during the Second World War, it was commandeered and used as prisoner-of-war camp. After the war, the Gosfords sold the estate and eventually it was acquired by the Forestry Commission. It was, for periods, occupied as a hotel, barracks, and restaurant. Following a long period of neglect it is now being converted into apartments. Part of the attraction is that the castle is situated at the heart of **Gosford Forest Park**, comprising 240 hectares of diverse woodland and open parkland set in gentle, rolling, drumlin countryside. It was designated the first conservation forest in Northern Ireland in 1986, and a series of pleasant walks take you through forests of both deciduous and coniferous trees, some of which are 200 years old. Increasing, popular with campers, attractions include a deer park, a large collection of wildfowl in its numerous ponds, and a walled garden.

Gosford Forest Park.

The nearby town of **Markethill** developed under the patronage of the Achesons of Gosford. In 1804, Sir Charles Coote described it as, 'a thriving town, the property of Lord Viscount Gosford; a neat sessions-house and several good houses have been lately built; this town is the principal stage between Armagh and Newry, and here is a good inn.' The town grew during the nineteenth century due to the development of the road network and railway, facilitating the supply of linen goods. But the town was hit hard by a severe bout of typhus, the impact of the Great Famine, and the decline of the Gosford Estate. Many of the town's older buildings, including the courthouse and markethouse, were built around this time. The courthouse, built in 1842, was opened in 2000 as a community venue and restaurant. Recently renovated, there is also an interactive touch-screen facility, which gives some background history of Markethill and the surrounding area during the past millennium.

The Gosford family worshipped at the nearby Church of Ireland at **Mullabrack,** where some fine old monuments can be seen, including one to George Lambert, V.C. of the 84th Regiment, Adjutant to his Regiment. This officer was born in the village of Hamiltonsbawn, a mile away, and won the Cross in the Indian Mutiny. At Mullabrack too, Admiral Lord Charles Beresford V.C. spent many of his boyhood days, his father being Rector.

Located on the highest point of a complex drumlin hill, 6km west of Markethill, is **Carnavanaghan Passage Tomb**, long recognised as an important landmark in the area. It is known locally as 'The Vicar's Cairn', and it is thought that the name is derived from a local interpretation of the townland *Carn na Mhanaghan* 'the monks' cairn'. The cairn is over 4,500 years old, is roughly circular and measures 32m in diameter, standing over 4m high above the ground surface at the south. This cairn was greatly disturbed in the early nineteenth century by amateur archaeologists and treasure seekers. In the late eighteenth century, it was reported that a passage or chamber was uncovered, and in 1797, it was described as a conical mound of stones surrounded by a kerb. In the next few years, there are newspaper reports of the removal of enormous quantities of stone, but that nothing worthy of notice was found. However, there are reports of stones with concentric circles and rectangular marks being found. The cairn today is topped by a triangulation pillar, but there are no signs of any marked stones, nor any structural stones.

A few miles north of Markethill along the B78, is the village of **Hamiltonsbawn**. It gets its name from the bawn or castle of John Hamilton, who was granted lands here in Plantation days, and who died in 1633. He was buried in Mullabrack church where his monument can still be seen, partly destroyed by ill treatment during the rebellion of 1641. In 1724, the 'bawn' and demesne lands were purchased by Sir Arthur Acheson of Gosford. In 1728, when Jonathan Swift was visiting Sir Arthur, he considered founding a school at Hamiltonsbawn and installing his friend, the playwright Richard Brinsley Sheridan, as schoolmaster. As for Sir Arthur Acheson, he was considering a number of options according to Swift who wrote, 'The Grand Question Debated as to whether Hamilton's "bawn" should be turned into a Barracks or a Malt-House'. The bawn became a barracks in 1731 and its first occupants were two troops of horses. It probably remained in use until the start of the nineteenth century, because 250 French prisoners were taken from Kinsale, after the famous battle of Kinsale, to Hamilton's bawn in 1798.

Dean Swift must have been impressed by the hard-working people of Hamiltonbawn at the time, because he also wrote a humorous little poem about the village:

> Newry town for mice and rats,
> Armagh city for dogs and cats,
> Hamilton's Bawn that keeps no Sunday,
> For every day is an Easter Monday.

In 1804, Sir Charles Coote considered **Hamiltonsbawn**:

> a good sized and well built village, about three miles from Armagh; on this hill above the town are the ruins of a castle, which appear of great antiquity, and to the eye of an observer it must seem almost incredible, that this mutilated and decayed building was, but a few years ago, an established and regularly garrisoned barrack.

Hamiltonsbawn was, until 1933, connected to Armagh city by rail. The main surviving features of this line are a tall, three-arched underbridge near Jerrettspass; the entrances to the Lissmummon and Lough Gilly tunnels, of which the former was exactly one mile in length; the longest railway tunnel in Ireland; and the station building at Markethill. From 1897 until about 1919, a horse-drawn tramway operated from here to the mills at Glenanne, a distance of about three miles.

That long-abandoned line will always be remembered as the location for the worst disaster in Irish railway history. It was between Hamilton and Armagh, at the northern end of this line, that the horrific accident occurred on 12 June 1889. The site at which the actual impact occurred can still be clearly distinguished in the townland of Killuney. Armagh Sunday school had organized a day trip to the seaside resort of Warrenpoint, a distance of about 24 miles. A special train was arranged for the journey, carrying almost 800 passengers. The route is steeply graded and curved, and with the train greatly overloaded, the train crew decided to divide the train and proceed with the front portion to Hamiltonbawn station, leaving the second half of the train on the steep slope. Unfortunately, the detached carriages, having no independent breaking system, rolled back and crashed into an oncoming passenger train, before tumbling down an embankment. Eighty people, including twenty-three children were killed. It later emerged that many of the passengers in the excursion train had been unable to escape as the doors were locked; witnesses stated that this was done to prevent ticketless travellers joining the train after the ticket inspection.

Chapter 9

West from Newry

South Armagh is a completely different proposition from the more populated northern slice of the country. For years it has been known to outsiders, if at all, from news reports, and even today is often referred to as 'Bandit Country' or 'The Killing Fields'. Nevertheless, it is an area of outstanding natural beauty and sadly neglected, not only by tourists but by most people in Northern Ireland.

Newry is, for many people, the gateway to the magnificent countryside of South Armagh. The city of Newry, the fourth largest in Northern Ireland, although partly in Co. Armagh is historically more associated with Co. Down. The River Clanrye, which runs through the city, forms the historic border between the two counties. Newry was founded in 1144, alongside a Cistercian monastery, and is one of Northern Ireland's oldest settlements. The city sits in a valley, nestled between the Mourne Mountains to the east, and the Ring of Gullion to the south-west, both of which are designated Areas of Outstanding Natural Beauty. Newry also lies in the shadow of the Cooley Mountains to the south east.

The train journey from Portadown, passing as it does through Scarvagh, Poyntzpass to Newry, is one of the most picturesque in Ireland. It is also of great interest for those interested in railway architecture. **MacNeill's Egyptian Arch** is a railway bridge, completed in 1851, for the Dublin and Belfast Junction Railway Company and was the result of collaboration between engineer Sir John Macneill, and constructor, William Dargan. Dubbed the Egyptian Arch, by locals because of its resemblance to a Pharaoh's head-piece, the rail bridge passes over the Newry – Camlough Road. The bridge was selected for the design of the British one pound coin to represent Northern Ireland for 2006. MacNeill's bridge is located less than one mile along the line from the **Craigmore Viaduct**, which he also designed. The viaduct, which spans the Camlough River, consists of eighteen arches of 60ft span, the highest being 126ft, making it the highest via-duct in Ireland. Construction began in 1849 for the Dublin and Belfast Junction Railway, and it was formally opened in 1852.

Newry is very much a frontier town, lying as it does just a few miles from the border with the Irish Republic. The A1 takes you out of the city and then the traveller heads towards Slieve Gullion along the B113. To the west is **Ballymacdermott** mountain where there is a three-chambered horned cairn. The tomb consists of a court and three chambers, the chambers separated by jambs. The chambers are now roofless, but originally they had a corbelled roof. It is worth a visit, if only for the excellent views it offers of the Meigh plain and surrounding countryside.

▴Craigmore Viaduct.

Ballmacdermott
Court.

On the south-eastern slopes of Slieve Gullion is the ancient church of **Killevy**,
founded by St Monenna. St Monenna, otherwise known as Darerca or Blinne, who
died around 517, and chose a peaceful spot on the eastern slope of Slieve Gullion
for her foundation, one of the few known early Irish nunneries. Despite its idyllic
location, it was raided by the Norsemen who pillaged it from Carlingford Lough.
Though appearing to be one building, the remains that survive today are two
churches built back to back. The western church is the older of the two, with a
twelfth-century window in the east gable. The east church may be of fifteenth-cen-
tury date, though its northern doorway looks older, and may have been moved from
a position in the west gable of an earlier stone church on the site. The foundation of
a small rectangular building, just outside the early west doorway, is sometimes taken
as evidence of the former existence of a round tower, but there is no proof of this.
The holy well and rag-tree on the nearby hillside, is known as St Bline's Well. A large
granite stone to the north of the graveyard is reputed to mark St Monenna's grave.

A few miles further along the road is **Slieve Gullion Forest Park**. A 10km drive
around the slopes of Slieve Gullion, offers visitors spectacular views of the surrounding countryside. For walkers there is a mountain top trail to megalithic cairns and
lake, with stunning views across the Ring of Gullion, Mourne Mountains, Cooley
Peninsula, and Armagh Drumlins, and over 2,000 years of legend and history. For the
less energetic, a leisurely walk around the walled garden is a must, as is a 2km walk
through the mostly broadleaf, mature woodland, utilising trails on the lower slopes of
Slieve Gullion. The woodland comprises oak, ash, birch, beech, sweet chestnut, and
horse chestnut, in which was once part of the chambre demesne.

Above and opposite: Killevy church.

Slieve Gullion is the eroded remains of a Paleocene volcanic complex. It is surrounded by a ring dyke. Slieve Gullion has been shaped by glaciation, and exhibits a classic 'crag and tail' glacial feature. The 'tail', composed of glacial deposits, points south, ending at Drumintee. From Drumintee, the ascent of Slieve Guillion, along the spine, offers a magnificent panorama and one of the finest views in Ireland. The mountain itself is associated with many legends, including tales of Cúchulainn, Fionn, and their contemporaries. On the mountain top, are an extensive lake and two cairns. The larger is known to locals as, 'the Cailleach Biorra's House'. It was *Cailleach Biorra* who lured the legendary giant Finn McCool to swim in her lake, from which he emerged an old man. To the north is Camloch Mountain, to the west is Slievenacappel, and to the south are Slievebrack and Croslieve, in the vicinity of Forkill.

Above and opposite: Slieve Gullion.

A few miles past Slieve Gullion is **Forkill**. Today it has become something of a dormitory village, with extensive new housing largely out of character with the village. It retains its unique appeal however, and is an ideal site from which to explore the charms of South Armagh. George Scott, in his notes for the Ordnance Survey for 1837, dismissed the village: 'It contains about 10 1-storey houses, of which 4 are slated; 15 2-storey houses, 11 of which are slated. The only public buildings are a Methodist meeting house, market house and mill. The village is in a wild district of country and not very likely to improve.' In fact, by the second half of the nineteenth century, it had become an industrial village with a corn mill, a scutch mill, a hotel, a post-office, and several grocery and drapery shops.

It is, however, a beautifully situated village, with a good trout stream running through it. The village is in the midst of delightful mountain scenery, and near by is Glendhu, the Dark Glen, which offers one of the prettiest drives in Co. Armagh, with Slieve Gullion in the foreground, flanked by Carrickasticken Mountain and cairn-crowned Carrickbroad. You will also see several ruined towers, and the remains of eighteenth-century follies, built by local gentry. They have been described as 'picnic towers', to which the squires would resort with their friends and families.

A little further on from Forkill is **Jonesbourgh**. Roth Jones, the area's principal landlord in the early part of the eighteenth century, founded the village in 1706, in an area known in 1556 and in the seventeenth century, as *Baile an Chláir* 'settlement of the plan'. By the early eighteenth century the English name for the village was Four Mile House, or Jonesborough, while the Irish name continued in use throughout the nineteenth century by Irish speakers in the area.

Both Jonesbourgh and Forkill straddle the border, and only the change in road markings alert the traveller to the fact that they made have strayed into the Irish Republic. The weaving border has been synonymous with smuggling over the years, and only the goods vary depending on the fluctuating currencies on both sides of the border. As Richard Hayward wrote in his *Border Foray* in 1957:

> Lorry and car loads of dutiable goods pass to and fro over remote parts of this Border, for in recent times with tariff changes the traffic is two-way, and everything is timed and planned with military precision. Currently soap powders and razor blades pass southwards with much profit, and cigarettes are constantly changing with the fluctuating tide of varying tariffs and the inexorable laws of supply and demand.

South of Jonesbourgh is the **Moyry Pass**, also known as the 'Gap of the North'. The gap was a strategic route into the ancient kingdom of *Ulaidh*, from which Ulster takes its name, and remained under the control of the Irish until the very early seventeenth century. It has been pivotal in both history and folklore; it was here that Cúchulainn defended Ulster from the forces of Connaught. St Moyry Pass was, in 1600, the scene of a titanic struggle between the Crown forces, under Mountjoy and Hugh O'Neill, Earl of Tyrone. The Irish forces had constructed three lines of trenches, backed up with barricades of earth and stone at Moyry Pass. On the flanks, the Irish had made further earth and stone works, and twisted the branches of low-growing trees, in order to provide cover for themselves and prevent the English occupying the heights on either side of the Pass. On arrival from Dublin with an army, Mountjoy viewed Tyrone's elaborate defences with

Moyry Castle.

surprise: 'These barbarous people had far exceeded their custom and our expectation'. Mountjoy's objective was to re-establish a garrison at Armagh, which had been evacuated by the English Crown after the battle of the Yellow Ford two years earlier. On the afternoon of Thursday, 2 October 1600, the Irish advanced with pike and handgun, clashing with five regiments sent to face them by Mountjoy. After three hours of close fighting, the English forces fell back in confusion. An English counter-attack the following Sunday failed. Shortly afterwards dysentery spread amongst the English troops. In despair one of the English captains remarked on O'Neill's defences that, he never saw 'a more villainous piece of work, and an impossible thing for an army to pass without an intolerable loss'.

View from Moyry Castle.

Killnasaggart Pillar stone.

Left: Ballykeel Dolmen.

Below and opposite: Creggan church yard.

Then, unaccountably, O'Neill withdrew from the pass on 13 October, and four days later Mountjoy marched through without opposition. Mountjoy advanced towards Armagh, stopping to erect a fort he named Mountnorris, eight miles from the city. At the time, Mountjoy could not understand why O'Neill would voluntarily leave such a strong defensive position. The most likely explanation for O'Neill's withdrawal is that he was both short of ammunition and food, and feared a flanking attack on his rear from Newry. Moreover, most of his forces were composed of temporary, clan-based levies, who could not be kept together for long.

Moyry Castle was built in 1601, by Lord Mountjoy to secure the pass. The keep or tower remains is a very picturesque feature in the scenery. The castle is built on solid rock and is three stories high. There are musketry loopholes on each wall, except the north-facing wall. This wall held the fireplaces which protrude on the outside. According to Richard Hayward in his *Border Foray*:

Crossmaglen.

Here, in 1601, Lord Mountjoy decided to tame the powerful O Neills once and for all, and the first part of his plan was to clear the gap of the forests and woodlands of which the Irish warriors made such skilful and deadly use. This done he built the Moyry Castle, in conformity with his idea that every danger point of this kind must be protected by a 'little keepe' to-day, ruinous now but full of history. Three storeys high it stands, neatly and compactly sited on a small rocky boss, with pleasantly rounded corners pierced for musketry on the ground floor level. Much of the history of modern Ulster is hinged on this curiously comely little tower, and it can be said that the Flight of the Earls was almost born of the foundations of this small stronghold.

In the adjoining townland of Edenknappa, and only a short walk from Moyry Castle, is one of the earliest datable Christian monuments in Ireland, erected before the year 716. Locally, it is, known as **Kilnasaggart Pillar Stone** (The church of the Priest). It is a tall pillar stone, seven foot high, and inscribed with some Ogham script, crosses, most within circles, and a Gaelic inscription. The Pillar Stone stands at the northern edge of a double circle of graves, the outer ring of graves being larger in size than the inner ones, with the feet of the dead pointing towards the centre. The graves cannot be seen as they are completely covered in grass. At the base of the stone, there are some small stones with crosses engraved on them.

Staying on the Armagh side of the border, the main road heads suddenly north at Forkill, passing along the west side of Slieve Gullion, towards Bessbrook. Turning west along the B30, you head towards Sliver Bridge and Crossmaglen, passing **Ballykeel Dolmen**. Ballykeel differs from many dolmens, in that it has three portal stones, so is of a type known as a tripod dolmen. Known locally, as 'The Hag's Chair', there are distinct remains around the dolmen of a stone structure, a cairn or cist, which was at one time part of the tomb. During excavations, large quantities of shards representing various Neolithic pottery styles, were found. Particularly important were the fragments of three highly-decorated and elegant vessels found in the dolmen chamber. Writing about Ballykeel in his last letter of 3 April 1850, to the Belfast Gaelic scholar, Robert McAdam, local poet and scribe Art Bennett said, 'There is more Irish history in the rocks of Ballykeel than ever there was possessed in Belfast. It was cradled and nursed there and more than likely will never waken'. For thousands of years, this fine monument has been an element in the area's rich heritage and folklore, its ancient stones inspiring local tales of fairies, witches, and hags.

North of Silverbridge is the **Dorsey Entrenchment,** a large rectangular enclosure measuring about 4km in circumference, which was constructed at about the same time as Navan Fort. One of the few monuments in Northern Ireland which have been confirmed as Iron Age in date, the name of the earthworks comes from the Irish *dóirse* (doors), as the area served as the traditional gateway into Ulster. It is located on one of the main routes between Louth and *Emain Macha*, and the old coach road between Dublin and Armagh is supposed to have passed through the Dorsey. There seems little doubt that one of its functions was also to protect Ulster, as seen by the fact that its major defensive line, a high bank straddled by two deep ditches, is only found on the part of the enclosure facing to the south.

Back on the road to Crossmaglen, **Creggan** is the next stop. Creggan church, *an Creagan*, 'rocky place', is situated near the wooded banks of the Creggan River, north-east of Crossmaglen. The Church of Ireland graveyard is well-known locally for containing the burial vault of the Ulster chieftain family, the O'Neills. The present Church of Ireland church was built in 1758, and the tower was added in 1799. It may, however, be built on the site of an earlier church. It was recorded in the nineteenth century that the O'Neills and McMahons buried their dead in a vault under the altar, but this was only discovered by accident in 1973. The graveyard also contains the graves of several eighteenth-century Gaelic poets, including Art McCooey and Patrick MacAliondain. MacCooey was the most famous member of this group, and his fine poem, *Uir-chill a Creagain*, is written in the form of a dialogue between the poet himself and a fairy maiden, and it is said that it was composed whilst the poet was hiding in the O'Neill vault from English soldiers. He is lamenting the passing of the old Irish aristocracy and their patronage of the native arts, whilst the fairy seeks to lure him away to the delights of fairyland:

Left and below: Newtownhamilton

Bottom left: Camlough parish church.

Bottom right: Keady.

In the noble church of Creggan I lay down in sorrow last night

And with the rising of the morning a maiden awakened me with a kiss,

She had laughing bright cheeks and her hair shone like gold

And it was the health of the world to be looking at that queenly young woman.

Another noted burial is that of John Johnston, or Johnston, of the Fews, who died in 1759. He was the much-feared chief constable of the Fews. Johnston was determined to retain a firm grip on the local population. He established the village of Johnston Fews, which he hoped would meet with the same success as many of the similar foundations of his neighbours. Four fairs were granted to the village, but by 1740, it was described as a, 'very small village in the middle of wild country called the Fews, notorious for robbers', and by the beginning of the nineteenth century, it consisted of no more than six houses. The Johnston family's attempts to bring law and order to the district, which included the building of Fews Barracks, resulted in the famous couplet about them:

Jesus of Nazareth, King of the Jews,

Protect us from Johnston, the King of the Fews.

The area remained infamous for its isolation and lawlessness. According to Thomas Molyneux in the early eighteenth century:

We designed for Ardmagh, and went 16 miles towards it, mostly on the very wild mountains, ye Fews. These mountains are of a boggy, heathy soile, ye road thro' them of a rocky gravel; in all this way you meet but one house, and nothing like corn, meadow, or enclosures. We baited on them at the second house, which is called Blackditch, where is also a small foot Barrack, but without any soldiers. Here was miserable entertainment, not so much as tolerable grass within 2 mile of 'em. From hence 2 or 3 mile brings you to the end of the mountains, and then you enter into a pleasant enclosed corn country, which in 5 or 6 miles brings you thro' very good new made roads to Ardmagh.

A roads runs eastwards from Creggan for about four miles to the village of Ballsmill, and a little more than half-way to that place, is **Glassdrummond Lake.** It was here that the O'Neills built their castle, and long before that, a crannóg was constructed. Glassdrummond Castle was built some time in the sixteenth century, and was destroyed in 1642, by its occupant, Shane O'Neill, to prevent its use as a garrison by the Cromwellian troops stationed in Dundalk. Until about 1700, it was a picturesque ruin but is now distributed amongst many buildings in the vicinity.

A few miles to the west of Glassdrummond Lake is **Crossmaglen**. It is a market town with a square, and is the most southerly town in Co. Armagh. This is a typical market town with a large square – locals claim the largest in Europe – in which great fairs were held. In his *History of the Upper Fews*, published in 1838, John Donaldson gives a pocket history of the town:

> Cross, or Crossmaglen. This town is part of the estate of Thomas P Ball, Esq., and is situated on a rising ground on the road from Newry to Carrickmacross, which is here intersected by one of the roads from Dundalk to Castleblayney … By the census taken in 1814 it contained 46 houses and 254 inhabitants … Here formerly 10 fairs were held in the year, but they are now discontinued and a fair is held the first Friday in each month, when cows, horses, sheep, pigs, and beasts of every description are sold; and oats, oatmeal by retail, potatoes, beef, mutton, pork, poultry, butter, eggs, &c., in their season; with frieze, wool, flax, linen yarn, turners' and coopers' ware, crockery, fruit, brogues and other commodities. Pedlars also keep standings for the sale of soft goods, hardware, &c. A market is also held here each Friday, where all the aforesaid goods and merchandises are disposed of, excepting live stock, which are reserved for the fairs.

The district was once surrounded by extensive woods and was the haunt of Tories and outlaws. The fairs of Crossmaglen were formerly notorious for the undesirable characters that frequented them. Many of the songs and ballads associated with Crossmaglen reflect this circumstance, as for instance:

From Carrickmacross to Crossmaglen
There are more rogues than honest men.

About two miles to the west is **Lough Ross**, with a crannóg in the middle of it, and on this crannóg, the Rebellion of 1641 was hatched and the final plans prepared. Not far from this, is the very fine Ring Fort of Corlis, a name which means the Fort of the Little Rounded Hill, and in the middle of this fort, is a very good souterrain. From Corlis Fort it is possible to get a fine view of Lough, Patrick, Lough Peter, and Lough Kiltyban, stretching towards the north one after the other, and of Lough Muckno across the Border in Monaghan. Further to the north, near Cullyhanna, is Lisleitrim Lough, also with a fine crannóg in the middle of it, and on the hillside above this, is the splendid Fort of Lisleitrim, with no fewer than three well-defined rings or ramparts.

From Crossmaglen, you travel north along the B135 towards Cullyhana and Newtownhamilton. On the way is the megalithic tomb at **Annaghmare** –

Stonebridge.

Eanach Mar, 'the big marsh', has been described as one of the finest surviving court tombs in Northern Ireland. This tomb was built by early farming communities over 6,000 years ago. Located on a rocky knoll in a modern forestry plantation, and surrounded by low boggy ground, it is best approached along a path through the trees. The tomb, which is known locally as 'The Black Castle', has been used for burials at various times in the Neolithic Age, and is thought to have been used for unconsecrated burials in the more recent past. During excavation of the burial gallery chambers, Neolithic pottery, flint scrapers, and a very fine javelin head were unearthed. The tomb contained the skeletal remains of an adult female and a child, and a great deal of cremated bone. 'The Black Castle' has been the site of many local ghost sightings.

Travelling north you pass through Cullyhanna, before reaching **Newtownhamilton.** The area was originally known as Tulivallen, but now takes its name from Alexander Hamilton, a descendant of the John Hamilton from Scotland, who founded Hamiltonsbawn. By 1814, it contained 165 houses and nearly 700 inhabitants. According to the *Ordnance Survey Memoirs*, 1838, Newtownhamilton quickly became a major market town for the region noted for its hiring fairs:,

> There is a fair held in the town on the last Saturday of every month which is pretty well attended, but the largest fair is on the last Saturday of the month of November and on the last Saturday in May which are termed "hiring fairs" where hire servants are engaged till next fair. The town on those day is crowded to excess and for some market days after it, for when the servants who are hired on fair days, when on going to their place they find it not so agreeable as they expected, they then come the following market day to look out for another master.

The ruined church of **Ballymoyer**, three miles north-east of Newtownhamilton, which is now almost completely clothed in ivy, was built in the seventeenth century, but probably replaces a much earlier structure. It continued to be in use until its replacement in the nineteenth century. It is a rectangular building, with a double bell-cot on the west gable and a doorway in the west wall. There are some round-headed windows. The name Ballymoyer is derived from *maor*, 'keeper' of the *Book of Armagh*, a position held by the MacMoyer family, first mentioned in Archbishop Sweetman's Register in 1367. In 1681, the head of the MacMoyer family, Florence MacMoyer, along with three clerical friends, conspired to slander Archbishop Oliver Plunkett, who had ruled against them in a clerical dispute. In order to pay for his journey to London, where the Archbishop was being held,

Florence MacMoyer pledged the *Book of Armagh* for £5. Upon his return to Ireland after the execution of the Archbishop, MacMoyer was unable to redeem the precious book, which eventually came into the hands of the Brownlow family in Lurgan.

From Newtownhamilton, the A29 heads east back towards **Newry**. It is worth stopping of at **Camlough**, from which Newry derives its water. Newry in its heyday was very much a canal town, and it is the canal, completed in 1742, that was a major impetus for industrial growth in many of Co. Armagh's towns, including Tandragee and Portadown, until the arrival of the railways a century later. Sadly derelict now, when it was a bustling thoroughfare it connected the city with the fertile agricultural land and busy mills of Co. Armagh all the way to Lough Neagh. The canal had a total length of 18½ miles with 13 locks, including those at Poyntzpass and Whitecoat Point where it joined up with the River Bann at Portadown and finally Lough Neagh. For those with a little time to spare, and who fancy a little exercise, the **Newry Towpath route**, which stretches from Newry Town Hall to the Bann Bridge at Portadown, a distance of twenty miles, is a great way to appreciate the unique beauty, and industrial and archaeological history of Co. Armagh.

Leabharlanna Poibli Chathair Bhaile Átha Cliath
Dublin City Public Libraries

Select Bibliography

Bassett, George Henry, *The Book of County Armagh* (Dublin, 1888).

Brett, C.E.B., *Buildings of County Armagh* (Belfast, 1999).

Bryans, Robin, *Ulster: A Journey through the Six Counties* (London, 1964).

Coote, Sir Charles, *Statistical Survey of the County of Armagh* (1804, reprinted 1984).

Hanna, Denis, O'D, *The Face of Ulster* (London, 1952).

Hayward, Richard, *In Praise of Ulster* (Belfast, 1938).

Hughes, A.J. and Nolan, W. et al, *Armagh – History and Society* (Geography Publications: 2001).

Lewis, S, *Topographical Dictionary of Ireland* (London, 1837).

Mallory, J.P., *Navan Fort, The Ancient Capital of Ulster* (Belfast).

Maxwell, Ian, *Researching Armagh Ancestors* (Belfast, 2000).

McCorry, Francis X, *Journeys in County Armagh and Adjoining Districts* (Lurgan, 2000).

McCreary, Alf, *Saint Patrick's City: The Story of Armagh* (Belfast, 2001).

McKinstry, *The Buildings of Armagh* (Belfast, 1992).

Ordnance Survey Memoirs: Parishes of County Armagh (Belfast, 1990).

Paterson, T.G.F., *Harvest Home, The Last Sheaf* (Armagh, 1975).

Rogers, E, *Topographical Sketches in Armagh and Tyrone* (1874).

Sherman, Hugh, *Ulster* (London, 1949).

Stuart, James, *Historical Memoirs of the City of Armagh* (Newry, 1819).

Weatherup, D.R.M., *Armagh, Historic Photographs of the Primatial City* (Belfast, 1990).